SOUTHERN AFRICA

The Year of the Whirlwind

'The storm has not struck yet. We are only
experiencing the whirlwinds that go before it. '
J. B. Vorster, Prime Minister of South Africa.
New Years' Day Speech, 1977

COLIN LEGUM

Africana Publishing Company
New York

First published in the United States of America in 1977 by
Africana Publishing Company
a division of
Holmes & Meier Publishers, Inc.
101 Fifth Avenue
New York, New York 10003

Library of Congress Cataloging in Publication Data
Legum, Colin.
  Southern Africa.

  1. Africa, Southern—Politics and government—1975-
2. Nationalism—Africa, Southern. 3. Africa, Southern—Foreign
relations. I. Title.
DT746.L43   1977   320.9'68   77-6264
ISBN 0-8419-0318-2

PRINTED IN GREAT BRITAIN

CONTENTS

INTRODUCTION

The crisis in southern Africa is rapidly moving towards a climax. It is now possible to predict that before the end of 1978 further decisive changes will have occurred in the power-structure of the region, producing important shifts in the whole of Africa's international relations. These changes could be at least as momentous as those which followed the collapse of the old Portuguese political system in April 1974.[1] The capitulation of Lisbon's rule in Africa had a number of consequential changes.[2] First, the effective power of the remaining white-ruled countries (Rhodesia, SA and Namibia) was seriously weakened. Second, the forces of violence grew in strength and importance—both from the side of the black challengers and from that of the white defenders. Third, two Marxist-Leninist regimes of a character quite different from anything previously seen in the continent replaced Portuguese rule in Mozambique and Angola, the two front-line neighbours of SA and Namibia; their emergence radicalized black attitudes both in the region and in other parts of the continent. Fourth, the Soviet bloc's influence increased in southern Africa, as exemplified by the Russian-Cuban military intervention in Angola and by the first visit—in April 1977—of a top USSR leader, President Nikolai Podgorny, to the area south of Zimbabwe river.[3] Fifth, the policy alterations of the Western nations—especially of its leading member, the US—were more significant than any other development since the Union of South Africa's creation in 1910.

This reorientation of Western policy was signalled by the speech made by the then US Secretary of State, Dr Henry Kissinger, in Lusaka in April 1976, almost two years to the day after the defeat of Salazarism.[4] Kissinger's sharp reversal of US policy—with its promise of support for 'majority rule' throughout southern Africa—reflected American understanding of the decisive shift of power which had taken place in the sub-continent. His motive in announcing this sea-change in his own policies was to resist the expansion, as he saw it, of Soviet influence in Africa. The Carter Administration—though no less concerned than Kissinger about the balance in world power—brought with it a new American commitment to the ideal of human rights. This new US approach made it more difficult for Britain to pursue its ambiguous policies, especially towards SA. A Labour Government, however preoccupied with the worst economic crisis in modern British history, found itself increasingly under pressure to keep pace with Washington. In response to this pressure, a new concept of Anglo-American co-operation in southern Africa was developed, matching what still remained of British influence with US strength. The sad death of Tony Crosland brought to the Foreign Office not only the youngest incumbent ever to hold that position, but also a man as committed to human rights as Carter's new team of policy-makers. Dr David Owen's initiative, launched just a year after Kissinger's Lusaka speech, showed a spirit previously lacking in British policy. The question is whether it has come too late.

This new Anglo-American approach to southern Africa's problems also influenced thinking in the European Community. One result was the establishment in May 1977 of the 'Contact Group' of five Western nations (the US, UK, West Germany, France and Canada) to try and persuade the Vorster regime to abandon its 'Turnhalle approach' to Namibia's independence. Significantly, the US member of the group is Don McHenry, a black diplomat and prominent critic of apartheid who

4

wrote an important study of US firms in SA.[5] The group's central concern has been to get agreement for free elections in the territory before any independence constitution is drafted, and to ensure Swapo's full participation in the independence process.[6]

Although the West's diplomatic stance towards SA has changed significantly, its economic involvement in the apartheid Republic still shows little sign of lessening; nor is there yet a readiness by those who help to strengthen SA's armed forces—notably France—to join in a complete military embargo. Nevertheless, if the present diplomatic initiatives over Rhodesia and Namibia should fail, it appears inevitable that Western awareness of the importance of dissociating itself from SA will also produce important changes to those aspects of its policies.

Meanwhile, the changed perceptions of Western interests in Africa have made a deep impact on SA thinking. The Republic's abiding fear for years has been that it would one day find itself isolated in the world community, and abandoned by its 'friends' in the West at a time of serious danger. In 1976, for the first time ever, the Republic's leaders began to acknowledge openly that the country would have to fight alone in the event of a violent conflict on its borders or inside the country. Speeches made by the State President, Dr N. Diederichs, and the Prime Minister, John Vorster, warned that the besieged Republic could no longer count on Western support. It would be hard to over-estimate the traumatic effects that recognition of this reality—so long denied or repressed—will have on white SA thinking. It represents, in the full sense of the term, 'a watershed' in the Republic's affairs. Indeed, the recognition of SA having reached a watershed in 1976 has become a recurrent theme in the speeches of the Republic's leaders.

SA's response to this new threat to its international relations was of two kinds: to strengthen its military defences against the storms ahead; and to intensify its diplomatic efforts to win back support in the West and, as a necessary condition for this, to regain the initiative in seeking 'detente' with Black Africa after the disastrous military intervention in Angola. However SA knows—but still finds it hard to accept—that its international relations are very largely determined by its internal conditions. Few nations in the world today want to be seen as friends of apartheid; but so long as the regime appeared to be 'stable'—and was able to offer attractive opportunities for international economic investment—its trading partners would be loath to go beyond moral condemnations of the iniquities of Separate Development. The urban black protest, which was triggered off by the student demonstrations in Soweto on 16 June 1976, destroyed the illusion of stability. Furthermore, the total international boycott against recognition of the Transkei Republic's 'independence' in October 1976 showed that, however much the Vorster regime still believes in Separate Development as a solution for its race problems, the world community has already come to take a different view.

SA is no longer seen, either inside or outside the Republic, as a formidable and granite-like fortress that can be relied upon to withstand the winds of change in Africa, or the external challenges that might come from anti-Western forces with an interest in demolishing the last 'bastion of the Western defence system' in the continent. This concept of SA as a 'Western bastion' was projected largely by the rulers in Pretoria, although it had (and still has) some adherents in Nato. However, Western political leaders like Kissinger have increasingly come to see that the real threat to their interests in Africa comes from buttressing apartheid. This realization of the political dimension of the West's strategic interests has come late. But it is certain to mean far greater Western effort in trying to recapture political influence with Black Africa at a time when the Soviets have begun to appear as a potentially strong ally of the liberation forces in southern Africa. Thus the prospect is of much greater Western pressures against SA in pursuit of a different order of priorities. The West, as one prominent Afrikaner put it bluntly, wants to 'back the winning horse', and it knows that the winner is not going to be tainted by apartheid.[7]

SA's greatest challenge will come, though, not from external forces but from its inability to cope with the internal social contradictions created in pursuit of apartheid. The urban black revolt and the widespread internal opposition—from both blacks and whites—to independent Bantustans are but two examples of these sharpening internal contradictions. There has for some years been talk about the urgent need for 'change' in the Republic. The fact that the need for change is so widely recognized (even by the country's ruling party) has been interpreted, especially in Western circles, as though it had already begun. But while change is 'in the air', it is not yet 'on the ground'. What became crystal-clear in 1976 was that the kind of changes in 'petty apartheid' which have been either introduced or offered by the Vorster regime, stop well short of dismantling Separate Development; and that the great majority of black South Africans, as well as a substantial section of white South Africans, will insist that the abandonment of Separate Development is itself an essential prerequisite for meaningful and acceptable change. What has also become clear is that even if a strong leader like Vorster wished to set a new course away from Separate Development, his white electorate would jettison him sooner than accept any fundamental changes in the *status quo*. This is the nub of the dilemma that faces the Republic at this dangerous moment in its history.

The social, economic and political forces that have helped to shape SA's present inequitable society have also placed its ruling class in a straitjacket from which it appears to be unable to escape for so long as political power is held exclusively in white hands. Yet if the country is to avoid revolutionary and violent change, it must somehow find a way of breaking free from its present rigid political constraints. For the first time in 1976, voices were heard suggesting a radical change in the Republic's system of government. Some—who saw the danger but still misread the nature of the forces now engaged—suggested adopting a counter-revolutionary authoritarian system to establish a tough dictatorship. Others began to talk about a 'benevolent authoritarian regime' which would be able to act decisively in re-distributing power within a new federal system. Even the possibility of a military regime was seen as one likely alternative. Vorster himself gave his support to a possible reform whereby a strong Executive President would assume the functions of the Prime Minister; but he still insisted that such a President must remain closely associated with an elected parliament. What is significant about this debate is the awareness it shows of the problems that have already arisen from the inflexibility of the present political system which makes it difficult, if not impossible, to respond to the developing internal crisis.

The developments in southern Africa have also brought new challenges to the independent Black States. In 1958 the late President Kwame Nkrumah said that Africa would not be liberated until the whole of the continent was free. Now that the whole continent is free—except for Djibouti and the three States in southern Africa—commitment to the struggles in Rhodesia, Namibia and SA has become a major preoccupation of the OAU. It is the first priority for the five so-called Front-line African States—Tanzania, Zambia, Mozambique, Botswana and Angola. Their role is discussed at some length in a later section, but what must be stressed is the strong preference they show, even at this late stage, for a peacefully negotiated settlement of the problems of southern Africa, rather than for a violent struggle. So long as they see any hope of a negotiated settlement for any of the three crisis countries, they are ready to engage in diplomatic initiatives such as those proposed by Dr Kissinger and Dr Owen. But until these negotiations can be shown to be successful, they will continue to help strengthen the forces of the armed struggle. The great majority of African leaders have no ideological commitment to the importance of an armed struggle as a condition for national liberation. For them, the path of revolutionary violence remains a less-preferred second choice. In pursuing their first choice they see their best hope as lying with the Western nations; and in pursuing their alternative course, they see their best—perhaps only—hope in relying on the military support (hopefully without political strings) of the Communist world. Reliance on either East or West makes it more difficult for them to ensure that the struggle over southern Africa is not internationalized, with the serious risk of direct or indirect intervention by the major Powers. In addition, they all share a strong interest in wishing to see a quick end to the crisis situation in southern Africa, since its continuation imposes serious and growing economic burdens on the Front-line States, as well as serving to destabilize the African political system. Even the professed revolutionaries among their number need, at this time, a period to consolidate their own recently-won and still far from secure political bases.

Finally, it is important to focus attention on Nigeria's role. The US Ambassador to the UN, Andrew Young, has described Nigeria as 'the most important country in Africa'. There is much truth in his observation—especially now that the present regime has at last begun to develop a significant policy and role for itself in Africa commensurate with its size and economic strength. The country has the kind of muscle which most other black countries still lack. It has really begun to move from largely rhetorical to more meaningful support for the liberation struggle in the sub-continent, while its backing for the Front-line Presidents could be of crucial importance. Speaking to the UN General Assembly in October 1976, the Foreign Minister, Brigadier Garba, served notice on multinational firms that the time was coming when they would have to choose between their interests in SA and Black Africa. Should Nigeria follow up on this warning, it could make a considerable impact on Western decision-making. It is also significant that Nigeria has offered to host the UN conference to discuss 'concrete action to isolate the SA regime', promote collective security against acts of aggression by the SA regime, and assist the liberation movements in southern Africa. The conference will be held in Lagos from 22-6 August 1977 and could become another landmark in modern African history.

NOTES

1. See Colin Legum: *South Africa: The Secret Diplomacy of Detente.* Rex Collings, London, 1975.
2. See Colin Legum: *Vorster's Gamble for Africa: How the Search for Peace Failed.* Rex Collings, London, 1976.
3. See Colin Legum and Tony Hodges: *After Angola: The War over Southern Africa.* Rex Collings, London, 1976.
4. For Dr Kissinger's speech, see Documents at end of this volume.
5. Don McHenry: *The Role of US Firms in SA*; Study Project on The Role of Foreign Firms in SA. Africa Publications Trust, London 1976.
6. See David Martin in *The Observer,* London; 15 May 1977.
7. Cas de Villiers, Director of Association International: *Afrika Instituut Bulletin,* Pretoria; Vol. 16, Nos. 9 & 10, 1977.

Africa in this decade is a testing ground of the world's conscience and vision. That blacks and whites live together in harmony and equality is a moral imperative of our time. Let us prove that these goals can be realized by human choice, that justice can command by the force of its rightness instead of by force of arms. These are ideals that bind all the races of mankind. They are the mandate of decency and progress and peace. This drama will be played out in our own lifetime. Our children will inherit either our success or our failure. The world watches with hope and we approach it with confidence. So let it be said that Black people and White people working together achieved on this continent—which has suffered so much and seen so much injustice—a new era of peace, well-being and human dignity.

PROLOGUE

Such were the visions and dreams of the great Afro-American educationist James Aggrey in the 1930s; of the Nobel prize winner Chief Albert Lutuli in the 1950s; and of the martyred Martin Luther King in the 1960s; but these words did not come from any of them: they were spoken by the US Secretary of State, Dr Henry Kissinger, in the Zambian capital, Lusaka, on 25 April 1976. He did rather more than paint dreams of the future; he committed America's influence, if not its power, 'to help achieve human equality in southern Africa' but without resorting to war. Kissinger's eloquence—and the momentous implications of this change in US policy—left his host, President Kenneth Kaunda, weeping openly. Less prone to public emotion, Tanzania's President, Julius Nyerere, quipped: 'Whenever I have thought about the future of South Africa I have always prayed to God and to Washington; now Washington has answered my prayers.'

Nobody supposed that Kissinger himself had undergone a Pauline conversion on the road to Lusaka producing the American commitment to the pursuit of majority rule in Rhodesia, Namibia and SA.[1] It was clearly necessary for Metternich's disciple to reverse his 1970 stand favouring the temporary expedient of helping maintain the political balance in southern Africa in favour of the white minority regimes. Obviously he needed to bring the US closer into step with the historical fact that that balance had shifted irreversibly with the collapse of Portuguese colonialism in April 1974.[2] That shift had taken place against the main thrust of Western policies; and Kissinger needed urgently to restore the West-East balance of influence in the area as it existed before the successful intervention of the Russians and Cubans in Angola in 1975.[3] Western policies in southern Africa were in shreds, and Kissinger was there to offer something new. African leaders were far less inclined to question Kissinger's motives than to evaluate the sincerity of his commitment. In the words

8

of Tanzania's President, Julius Nyerere: 'I believe Dr Kissinger is right in saying, if you want to work for American interests—or Western interests in southern Africa—throw your weight on the side of those who are working for majority rule. If you don't and the war goes on, we have said, we can't give these people arms to fight; they will achieve their independence only through the support which they get from the Communist countries, and this is not in the interests of the Western Powers. So I suppose he is right in doing this, but I am saying, so what? I want his pressure. I want American pressure. I want American pressure on the side of majority rule. And I have no intention of quarrelling with the Americans. What I'm interested in is majority rule in southern Africa.'[4]

Kissinger had made his debut on the African stage just a month after the African Front-line Presidents (FLPs)—Julius Nyerere of Tanzania, Kenneth Kaunda of Zambia, Samora Machel of Mozambique and Sir Seretse Khama of Botswana—had apparently given up all hope of a peaceful settlement in Rhodesia, and so committed themselves in public to support for total armed struggle. They had reached their decision only with deep misgivings. So when Kissinger suddenly appeared in his new role, they were willing to receive him—not as a diplomatic wizard, but as a possible *deus ex machina* who, even at this late an hour, might just succeed in helping either to prevent a disastrous war, or at least to limit its scope by discouraging international involvement in the struggle over Rhodesia and Namibia.

Whatever their reservations, the African leaders' policy (as exemplified by that of the FLPs) was a dual one. First, they aimed to end minority rule in Rhodesia and Namibia and subsequently also in SA, and to do it quickly; and if at all possible to achieve the transfer of power with a minimum of violence and economic dislocation, thus avoiding revolution. Second, they were committed to support an armed struggle in the last resort if peaceful methods should prove unavailing; and, even if it came to war, they hoped to resist external military involvement of any kind on African soil. However, this latter objective was modified in one major respect during the Angolan struggles: a majority of African States adopted the position that SA military intervention in a neighbouring country justified an African Government inviting the help of a friendly superpower. This African concensus on the legitimacy of foreign military intervention is specially relevant to possible future developments in Rhodesia, Mozambique and Namibia.

Two parallel developments in southern Africa interacted strongly with each other throughout 1976 and the early part of 1977. One was the steady build-up for war—with the guerrillas emerging as a credible force, and the white minority regimes adding heavily to their defence capacity. The other was energetic diplomacy to avert the war. The African leaders most directly involved in the confrontation, the FLPs, backed both courses of action simultaneously. They wanted diplomacy to succeed, but they feared it would not; they worked for peace, but prepared for war, as many others have done. Their pessimism grew out of their doubts about the willingness of Western leaders to exert irresistible pressures on Smith's government which they believed was the only way of producing a negotiated settlement. These pressures it seemed could be applied quickly and effectively only through SA's commitment to them. But while the Prime Minister, John Vorster, favoured a peaceful settlement in Rhodesia, he seemed unwilling to apply the necessary pressures on the Smith regime. Therefore, the crucial question for the FLPs was whether the British and Americans could or would turn the screws on Vorster. There seemed little doubt that SA could break white Rhodesia's resistance by turning off their arms and fuel supplies. The question was how to induce them to do so. Again, in Nyerere's words: 'SA supports Smith. Without SA, Smith is not likely to last for very long. The Americans have the necessary power to say to the South Africans, "You are the supporters of Smith, stop supporting Smith or else".[5]

Nyerere and his presidential colleagues accept that 'you can believe Vorster—he's quite serious when he says that he wants this war to come to an end as quickly as possible . . . because if the war goes on very long, the government which takes over is going to be a more radical government and is going to be more committed to continuing the revolution in southern Africa.'[6] But they also believe that Vorster's problems with his own white electorate would make him reluctant to do what was necessary unless forced to do so. Nothing that happened before Kissinger's shuttle had encouraged them to think that the Americans or British were prepared to act decisively, notwithstanding that it was as much a Western as an African interest to avoid a damaging war in southern Africa. There was just a chance, they felt, that if the guerrillas' challenge in Rhodesia were taken sufficiently seriously in London and Washington—and especially if it looked as though the Russians and Cubans might become involved as their principle allies—that this might become the necessary incentive for a tough Western response to force the collapse of the Smith regime. This, then, was another reason for committing themselves finally to the armed struggle in February 1976. Before taking this step the FLPs had done all that seemed possible to achieve the goal of majority rule in southern Africa by diplomatic methods. They had even accepted to work with 'the devil himself'—John Vorster—in negotiations begun in 1974 and pursued throughout 1975[7] in the hope of achieving two results: to get Smith to negotiate with the Zimbabwe leaders to achieve a peaceful settlement in Rhodesia; and to induce the SA Government to negotiate with the South West African People's Organization of Namibia (Swapo). But these negotiations had led nowhere; and after SA's military intervention in Angola it was no longer possible for the FLPs to keep up their direct contacts with Pretoria. A complete gulf had again opened up between white and black Africa. That gulf, it seemed, might be bridged by Kissinger. Thus his intervention was unhesitatingly accepted when he signalled his readiness to become involved.

THE ROAD TO WAR: JANUARY-APRIL 1976

The sudden end to four centuries of Portuguese colonialism in Africa in April 1974 had opened a remarkable chapter in African history. It began with Vorster's immediate recognition that SA had to adjust to a new balance of power in the subcontinent. It continued with the ready response of the African Front-line Presidents to accept his offer to talk about peaceful ways of settling the crises in Rhodesia and Namibia, as a prelude to tackling the infinitely more difficult problem of apartheid itself.[8] The high point of this initiative to achieve peaceful change was the meeting at the Victoria Falls in August 1975 between the Smith regime and his black challengers, with Vorster and Kaunda in close attendance.[9] But their attempt to get white and black Rhodesian leaders to meet around the conference table failed; by the beginning of 1976 only one nationalist leader, Joshua Nkomo, was still trying to negotiate. Most of the other black Rhodesian leaders were in exile, either voluntarily or to avoid arrest, where they were keeping up a pretence of unity under the umbrella of the African National Council (ANC).[10] Its top leaders at that time, Bishop Muzorewa and Ndabaningi Sithole, were in fact united only in their criticism of Nkomo's attempts to arrange a 'deal' with Smith. Sithole's own position as the leader of the Zimbabwe African National Union (Zanu) was under strong challenge from Robert Mugabe, who had led a move to depose him while they were still in prison together in Salisbury. Mugabe had from the first refused to co-operate with the ANC, or to have anything to do with the FLPs' moves for a peaceful settlement. He believed only in the armed struggle, and he devoted himself to organizing the 20,000 or more young black Rhodesians who had crossed into Mozambique after the Frelimo Government achieved its independence in July 1975. This spontaneous exodus was to become a crucial turning-point in the Rhodesian struggle. It brought an infusion of new blood into the guerrillas' ranks with demands for younger leaders in place of the old politicians. Only Mugabe found general acceptance among the Zanu cadres. Nkomo, by continuing to negotiate with Smith, was taking considerable risks to outmanoeuvre his rivals for power; but he did not share Kaunda's view that he would become 'irrelevant' if the negotiations ended up in failure. He was too shrewd a politician to leave himself without a strong fall-back position, and he lost no opportunity to make it clear that his stand was 'negotiate or fight'. At that time, Zapu had few battalions of its own in the guerrilla camps—perhaps 800 to 1,000; but still enough to give Nkomo a place in the guerrilla struggle.

Positions within the black Rhodesians' camp at the beginning of 1976 can be summed up as follows. The ANC had lost most of its coalition character; Bishop Muzorewa was no longer accepted as the unifying chairman, but could still rely on the support of some of Nkomo's former lieutenants, like James Robert Chikerema and George Nyandoro, and on a popular base at home. Ndabaningi Sithole had resuscitated Zanu in exile and while strongly championing the armed struggle, was rapidly losing ground to Mugabe who was quietly beavering away in the Mozambique bush. All these rival elements were suspicious of, and hostile to, Nkomo's continuing efforts to negotiate with Smith. Nkomo ran the risk of isolating himself from the external movement, but not from the FLPs; Kaunda, in particular, encouraged him to persevere for so long as there was any hope of an agreement.

All these old and new divisions in the Zimbabwean ranks seriously weakened, and even discredited, the black nationalist position. They also weakened the FLPs' attempts to apply pressures on Britain and SA to play a more vigorous role in Rhodesia.

By February 1976, it was clear that the last black pawn in play was held in checkmate by white knight. Nkomo was preparing to change his strategy; he was beginning to sound just like the other black militants fully committed to the armed struggle. But Nkomo was alone in expressing his views inside Rhodesia. Smith, the grandmaster of defence, had once again succeeded in scuppering the talks into which he had reluctantly been forced by Vorster. Having previously passed up two opportunities for settlement with the British, he was still relying on the strategy that had served him so well in the past: buying time with which to wear down his opposition, and living on the hope that at the end of the day, SA and the US would be driven by their own interests to back him. But in the meantime, African patience had begun to run out. The FLPs, at a crucial meeting in Quelimane (Mozambique) from 7-8 February, unanimously decided that nothing more could be expected from their current efforts to achieve change by peaceful methods; they now declared their unqualified support for an armed struggle. To mark this change in their policy they also decided to withdraw their support from all the Zimbabwean political leaders and parties, and to give their backing to the Joint Military Command formed three months earlier in the camps which had been set up to weld the guerrillas into the Zimbabwe Independent People's Army (Zipa).

Kaunda and Nyerere met at Mbale, southern Tanzania, on 21 February to try and reconcile their differences over Angola, and also to discuss how to get Britain and the US to appreciate how serious the position had become in Rhodesia with the impending collapse of the Smith-Nkomo negotiations and with the FLPs' decision to support the militants. Kaunda sent his envoy, Mark Chona[11] to London, Bonn and Washington to impress on the leaders there the full import of the Quelimane decision. At the same time he published a warning intended to achieve two purposes:[12] he wanted the Western community to understand the reasons for the African stand in opting for the armed struggle; and he still hoped to induce Britain and the US to recognize how close the sub-continent was to war, which could only be averted by immediate Western leverage on Smith and Vorster. Kaunda's published warning marked a new phase. He said: 'The Western countries should not blame anybody when the Angolan situation repeats itself in Zimbabwe, as the freedom fighters will turn to the Eastern bloc countries, the only ones willing and prepared to help them achieve their freedom . . . Due to Smith's intransigence, Zambia has reached the end of the road regarding negotiations as an instrument of change. We have discharged our obligations under the OAU manifesto on southern Africa. The Western countries have refused to extend a hand of friendship to us by responding positively in Rhodesia. The worst they have feared all along—the factor of Communism—must now inevitably be introduced in Zimbabwe because majority rule must now be decided on the battlefield.'

Replying to questions about how a violent struggle in Rhodesia would affect relations with SA, Kaunda replied: 'Our contact with SA was based on the resolution of political problems in Rhodesia and Namibia on the basis of majority rule and on the destruction of apartheid. It was never about economic co-operation. SA has not succeeded in her efforts to produce majority rule in Rhodesia. It must be understood that there can be no co-operation with the racist regimes without a common political denominator—the full realization of human rights. Zambia, by her principled stand and behaviour, invested all her resources at great expense, into peace programmes. But Zambia's efforts have not been reciprocated by support from those who have important interests in southern Africa. Therefore, the dreadful consequences which we have tried to avoid in this area must now come. Zambia should not be blamed. We have discharged our responsibilities to the international community.'

The FLPs' Quelimane decision left the British Government troubled but without any ideas about what effective policy to pursue on Rhodesia. It behaved like the captain in charge of a ship whose engines have been stopped by mutineers in heavy seas, and with the prospect of worse storms to come: it could issue urgent warnings about the dangers ahead, but seemed powerless to act. A few days after the Quelimane warning, the then Foreign and Commonwealth Office (FCO) Minister of State for African Affairs, David Ennals, disclaimed any British intention of going to the rescue of white Rhodesians: 'It should not be thought that, somehow or other, we would be committed to rescuing our kith and kin, who have shown such extraordinary neglect of responsibilities in Rhodesia.' This speech outraged many in the Tory Opposition; but on 19 February, Ennals affirmed that he was not just expressing his own views but also those of the then Foreign Secretary, James Callaghan. He then set out current official thinking about Rhodesia: 'The prospect of armed conflict . . . in what seems bound to be an escalating spiral of violence and bloodshed' had achieved a new dimension after Angola. 'It must surely be in the mind of Mr Smith and his colleagues that if the talks were to end and the battle begin in earnest, there could be no guarantee that there would not be significant and dangerous intervention from outside forces . . .'[13]

Britain made two diplomatic moves at the end of February to try and avert the collapse of the Smith-Nkomo talks. The first was to get the European Economic Community to declare itself on the issues of southern Africa: it affirmed 'the right of the Rhodesian and Namibian peoples to self-determination and independence;'

and condemned 'the apartheid policy of SA and all external military intervention in Angola or surrounding African countries'.[14] The second step was to send Lord Greenhill, a former head of the FCO, on a fact-finding mission to Salisbury. Greenhill warned white Rhodesians that their only hope lay in negotiating seriously about majority rule; the alternative would be war and, if it came, there could be no hope of any Western nations intervening on their side—even in the event of a Communist-backed invasion of Rhodesia.[15] Speaking for the Smith regime, the Cabinet Secretary Jack Gaylard replied that 'the only guarantee of future stability, prosperity and harmony in Rhodesia is to retain the reins of government in responsible hands. This does not imply there will be no changes, but it does mean that any request for an immediate handover to black rule is out of the question.'[16]

The ANC leaders in exile—still suspicious that Britain was engaged in a secret deal with Smith and Nkomo—denounced the Greenhill mission in a statement which rejected any further British role in Rhodesia. Their spokesman, James Chikerema, said: 'We have already declared war. We will not accept any settlement between Smith, Nkomo and the British Government.' Callaghan announced the failure of the Greenhill mission in Parliament on 2 March. The time had come, he said, for white Rhodesians to accept the 'inevitability of an early transfer of power to the black majority. Until they do, and until they recognize that this will come, either by negotiation or through guerrilla activity, I do not think we shall be able to proceed to further calculations about the future of Rhodesia.'

On the next day, 3 March, Mozambique closed its borders with Rhodesia. While this tightened the sanctions cordon, it also brought new problems for the Frelimo Government at a time when its own economic circumstances were little short of disastrous, and its capacity to defend its own borders completely inadequate.[17] This bold but risky step had previously been decided on by the FLPs at their meeting in Quelimane. The FLPs' thinking at that time was expressed by Nyerere in an interview with David Martin in early March[18] in which he repeatedly stressed 'the very real danger' of Britain trying to by-pass 'the Third Force'. 'I want the British to do two things,' he said. 'In the first place to do nothing in Rhodesia. And second, to support Mozambique in applying economic sanctions against Rhodesia.' He added that Britain had trusted the FLPs when they had gone to 'almost ridiculous lengths to give the talks a chance; now Britain should trust them with the second alternative (armed struggle). We are not enemies of Britain. We are building the pressure which will deliver Smith to London.' There was, he thought, 'a lot of hysteria in the West about Cuba in relation to Rhodesia'.

Precisely this anxiety was uppermost in Washington's thinking about Africa as it was in the ranks of the British Tories. In a parliamentary debate on 10 March, the Shadow Foreign Secretary, Reginald Maudling, put the blame on the Mozambique Government for 'conniving, if not fomenting, terrorism and bloodshed across the border of Rhodesia'. The Conservatives therefore opposed the British government's proposal to join with the UN in offering aid to Mozambique in compensation for the closing of its border.

The talks between Smith and Nkomo finally collapsed on 19 March. 'We have come to the end of the road,' Nkomo announced. Kaunda added: 'Africa must now help to intensify the armed struggle which is now in full swing'. And Smith, in a typically ambiguous statement, called on Britain to be prepared to 'resume its responsibilities for Rhodesia,' adding that he would be ready to consider a return to legality 'if I am satisfied, and it could be shown that this or any other decision is necessary in the interests of Rhodesia'. On 22 March, Callaghan set out Britain's terms for a settlement of the crisis.[19] He proposed two stages to independence. The first stage required acceptance of majority rule and elections within 18 to 24 months. The second stage would allow for negotiations about the independence constitution itself. There was to be no independence before majority rule. Thus the British Government firmly committed itself to the long-debated demand for a declaration on NIBMAR (No Independence Before Majority Rule) which, when it was first invented by Nyerere in 1966, almost blew the Commonwealth apart. Now, in 1976, with the war clouds rolling up over the Rhodesian veld and bush, Callaghan's reference to NIBMAR passed unnoticed. Once again, Callaghan's 22 March proposals had shown Britain as the captain of a mutinous ship—able to set a course, but with not the slightest idea of how to get the mutiny under control and so to get the ship moving along it. Nevertheless, Callaghan's speech was to have important, if at that time still unforeseen, results. It provided Kissinger with the clue he had been seeking to carry his personal diplomacy to Africa: the 22 March proposals were to become the basis for his Anglo-American initiative. But while he was planning that initiative, the dangers were continuing to mount. Callaghan sent Ennals to explain his proposals to the FLPs at the end of March. On his return to London at the beginning of April Ennals said that the African leaders saw no alternative but 'to fight to the finish'.[20] His conclusion was that unless white Rhodesians were willing to accept conditions for a peaceful settlement 'it seemed that a racial war could not be avoided, and although it might drag on for a long time there could be no doubt about its outcome'. The Foreign Office backed up this warning in replies to questions from the editor of the *Sunday Mail* (Salisbury) on 11 April. White Rhodesians were told that if Smith wanted to satisfy the British Government he would have to agree to 'a rapid and orderly transfer of power'; it was no longer enough just to accept the principle of majority rule. This amplification of Callaghan's 22 March proposals showed a new toughness in British thinking. Rhodesians were bluntly warned that the only alternative to a 'peaceful transition to majority rule in the very near future is an all-out war which the white Rhodesians cannot win'. However, the British Government continued to stand firmly by its original position taken at the time of UDI: it would not send troops to Rhodesia for any purpose. Kaunda had again called for British military intervention on 29 March to arrest Smith's rebels and to install a British-led executive committee composed of an equal number of whites and blacks to run the country for a year before holding free elections. On 31 March, Ennals told the House of Commons: 'Our position is absolutely clear. We were not prepared in 1965 to intervene militarily at the time of UDI and we would be no more prepared to intervene militarily today, either to take action supporting the minority against the majority or, as President Kaunda suggested, to arrest those now holding power.'

THE RINGMASTERS: THE ROLE OF THE FRONT-LINE PRESIDENTS

The four Front-line Presidents, joined by Angola's President, Agostinho Neto, in September 1976, have come to play a remarkable role in the continent's affairs, acting as a closely-knit caucus within the Organization of African Unity (OAU).[21] Although there is no formal approval for this role, the OAU has in fact endorsed all their major decisions to date. The original quartet emerged as a purely *ad hoc* group of like-minded leaders in response to Vorster's overtures in October 1974.[22] President Julius Nyerere of Tanzania and President Kenneth Kaunda of Zambia have for long been close friends and neighbours, who were linked in what was once known as the Mulungushi club. (Its third member was Milton Obote, President of Uganda until his overthrow in 1971. President Mobutu of Zaire, admitted in 1973, dropped out in 1975.) Nyerere and Kaunda are both on close terms with President Sir Seretse Khama of Botswana, who sees them as his principle allies in an effort to lessen his dependence on SA. Nyerere was especially close to President Samora

Machel of Mozambique, a friendship which grew out of Tanzania's long and courageous role in serving as the base country for Frelimo's struggle. However, there is a basic difference of outlook between them: Machel is primarily concerned that the independence struggle should itself help shape the revolutionary character of the emergent State; while Nyerere's concern during the independence struggle is simply to produce a representative black majority. A political and economic philosophy will be moulded according to the people's will after independence.

Nyerere's role as chairman of the FLPs was crucial, for although there were no fundamental differences within the group, there were times (as over Angola) when Kaunda and Machel were at odds. Machel is himself under constant pressures from his passionately revolutionary Marxist colleagues to abandon diplomacy, refuse to have any dealings with the 'Western Imperialists' and concentrate exclusively on the 'correctness of the armed struggle'. Only Nyerere had the trust of all the Frelimo leaders needed for the cooler diplomacy of negotiating with Kissinger and Vorster. Kissinger was anathema to the revolutionaries of Maputo—committed allies of MPLA—so it was no easy matter for Nyerere to persuade them to accept the Secretary of State's initial approaches to the FLPs. Nyerere's credentials as a champion of the liberation movements in southern Africa also give him the standing necessary to overcome criticisms about the FLPs 'usurping the functions of the OAU'. Such accusations were levelled over their decision to give exclusive recognition to the Patriotic Front and, even more sensitively, to adopt a strategy of priorities whereby the overthrow of apartheid in SA was to be dealt with only after Rhodesia and Namibia had been successfully tackled—a decision strongly challenged by the SA liberation movements. Nyerere justified this strategy to a critical audience of students at Ibadan University, Nigeria, on 17 November 1976, on these grounds: 'Compromise on the inessentials and a scale of priorities are unavoidable for African Governments and peoples. Our States and organizations have very limited resources; not every injustice or example of exploitation can be fought at once. Attempting to do so can be an invitation to disaster, and to the triumph of reaction.'

The frequent portrayal of Kaunda as a 'moderate' reluctantly being dragged along behind the militants is, as Nyerere has explained,[23] quite inaccurate. And, notwithstanding their different political attitudes, Machel regards Kaunda as 'a hero of the African liberation struggle'.[24] Without him, he said, Frelimo could not have succeeded. Kaunda was certainly reluctant about going to war; but then so were the others. Perhaps because he is by nature a moralist and a pacifist, he agonized more publicly than the others about his dilemma It is also true that he dared to hope longer than his colleagues that peaceful negotiations might be possible after all; thus he encouraged Nkomo to go on negotiating long after the rest had given up. Moreover Kaunda had been most closely involved with Vorster in the abortive negotiations of 1974-5, and had stood out to the end against endorsing the Russian-Cuban intervention in Angola. This made him especially vulnerable to accusations that he was engaged in making 'secret deals with the enemy'. These suspicions, voiced by some Swapo leaders and by the ANC of SA, were assiduously fed by the Russians. However, the truth is that Kaunda was fully in step with his colleagues on all the crucial issues touching on Rhodesia and Namibia.

Samora Machel's position was in some ways the most difficult of all. Throughout 1976 and early 1977 he was burdened with the problems of establishing the authority of his young government in a country overwhelmed by economic dislocation and by border and other security threats. Frelimo's leaders are personally divided over their commitment to a revolutionary ideology, as well as over the hard necessity of having to behave pragmatically in their relations with SA.

Machel is as divided inside himself as is his government over the contradictory demands of a revolutionary ideology and pragmatic realism, giving the impression that he might refuse to go along with the other FLPs. But whatever the revolutionary utterances of some of his lieutenants, Machel himself has proved a loyal colleague to the other Presidents.

Sir Seretse Khama is another of the misnamed 'moderates'. He surprised even his Presidential colleagues by the vigour of his support for policies likely to prove acutely embarrassing for Botswana's relations with SA—as over his support for armed struggle in both Rhodesia and Namibia. Despite Botswana's economic and military vulnerability, Khama never once dissented from any of the decisions taken by the FLPs. However, when the Front-line States began offering bases to the liberation movements, Botswana was specifically excluded. Otherwise, as Kaunda explained, 'it would be unfair. We want Botswana to consolidate because she is geographically in a very difficult position.'[25]

The latecomer, Angola's President Agostinho Neto, fitted least easily into the group when he joined in September 1976. Kaunda and Khama had both taken a strong stand against the MPLA's bid for power in 1975, and Zambia was among the last of the African States to recognize the MPLA government. But Nyerere and Machel had both supported Neto, and the Mozambique leader is one of the MPLA's closest allies; both believe in Marxist-Leninism. The FLPs needed Neto's close association if they were to play any effective role in Namibia. Neto, however, made no effort to disguise his disapproval of the FLPs' policy of co-operating with the 'imperialist' diplomatic initiative of Dr Kissinger (see below).

The FLPs' arena is southern Africa; their objective is to achieve majority rule, preferably through peaceful negotiations, but in the last resort by armed struggle. Their script is the Lusaka Manifesto of 1969 [26] written by Nyerere and Kaunda. Their authority as decision-makers has often been questioned, but never seriously challenged. Some countries in the area—like Lesotho, Kenya and Uganda —resented their exclusion from the charmed circle; but others with equal claims —like Malawi, Zaire and Swaziland—made no protest. The FLPs have had problems in handling their relations with other OAU members, particularly with regard to the liberation movements, and especially over the rivalries within Zimbabwe. Both the ANC and PAC of South Africa were also hostile to their dealings with Pretoria, particularly because FLP strategy leaves the issue of SA to be dealt with last. Some elements in Swapo's leadership, at their headquarters in Zambia, had their suspicions of a possible secret deal between Kaunda and Vorster as the price for settling Rhodesia; some even falsely suggested that Swapo's guerrillas had actually been denied active duty in 1976. The tensions within Swapo increased when Kaunda refused to give his exclusive backing to the MPLA which had become Swapo's closest ally after their former Angolan supporter, Unita, had accepted help from SA in 1975.

The ringmasters' most difficult act was to present the divided ranks of the Zimbabwean movement as a credible challenge to the Smith regime. They had impatiently tried to compel the leaders of Zanu, Zapu and Frolizi to unite under the chairmanship of Bishop Muzorewa in the ANC in December 1974—a facile unity which alienated Mugabe and offended Nkomo.[27] A year later they tried again. Withdrawing their support from all the rival politicians, they resolved to build up a 'Third Force'—the Joint Military Command of the Zimbabwe Independent People's Army (Zipa). Henceforth only the fighters were to be allowed to dictate the shape of the struggle. But when the scene was being set for negotiations in Geneva, the FLPs advised Britain to invite the groups led by Nkomo, the Bishop and Mugabe as well as the guerrilla leaders. Later they proposed that Sithole, too, should be asked to attend to avoid the impression that they were choosing the leaders for the Zimbabweans. During the first round of talks at Geneva in October, Muzorewa and Sithole both found themselves increasingly isolated by the Patriotic Front, an alliance of convenience newly-formed by the rivals, Nkomo and Mugabe. Muzorewa in particular lost out. Like the former French Prime Minister, Pierre Mendes-France in his political heyday, the Bishop could complain that everybody was against him 'except the people'. But whatever his popularity at home, he could not count on many guns in the camps—and at that late hour the struggle was seen to have shifted from the political arena to the battlefield. Muzorewa was understandably angry. One of his deputies, Dr G. L. Chavunduka, irresponsibly attacked Kaunda in public for 'plotting with Smith and the Western imperialists' to undermine him. The Bishop refused to apologize when asked by Lusaka to do so. Predictably he was disowned first by Kaunda and then by the other FLPs who, in November 1976, abandoned all attempts at neutrality and recognized the Patriotic Front as the political voice of the Third Force (Zipa). Thus the maverick Mugabe and the 'sell-out' Nkomo (the two men most offended by the FLP decision to recognize the ANC in 1974) emerged as the chosen; while the Bishop and Sithole, the beneficiaries of that original decision, were left out in the cold. The idea of coming down firmly on one side was Machel's. He had for long argued against allowing divisions within the struggle that could leave two armies fighting each other after independence, as had happened in Angola. What still remained uncertain was the degree to which Zipa itself was united in its support for the Patriotic Front. As late as January 1977, Mozambique's Foreign Minister, Joaquim Chissano, could only express 'hope' that the recognition of the Patriotic Front would strengthen 'unity within Zipa', because the 'lack of co-ordination at the political level had not inspired confidence in the fighters . . . We hope that the Patriotic Front will be recognized as the leaders of the armed struggle led by Zipa. This is a problem which will be discussed . . .'[28]

The FLPs did not always hold identical views about the different Zimbabwe leaders. Kaunda's preference was for Nkomo; he was alienated from Mugabe because of the latter's wild attacks on him. Machel had been the first to befriend Mugabe, at a time when he was completely alienated from Kaunda and Nyerere, because of his effectiveness in helping to organize the Zimbabwe refugees in Mozambique. Mugabe's single-minded commitment to the armed struggle had also won him many friends in Machel's circle. However, Machel came increasingly to support Nkomo, who was also favoured by Neto. Neither Nyerere nor Seretse Khama showed any particular preferences.

THE PERFORMERS: FIGHTERS AND POLITICIANS
The success of the FLPs in masterminding the political strategy against Rhodesia and Namibia depended entirely on the performance of Zimbabwe's politicians and fighters. In this they were badly let down. The political leadership's chronic disunity also inevitably hampered the effectiveness of the guerrilla struggle. The Zimbabwean leaders naturally blamed the FLPs for making their internicine quarrels worse; but, not surprisingly, the source of such attacks depended on who was in or out of favour with the Presidents at any particular time. These reversals of policy cannot be put down just to vacillation or lack of judgement; each change reflected shifts in the ranks of the Zimbabweans themselves. Mistakes were undoubtedly made: for example, Kaunda has admitted that in 1974 they had wrongly accepted Sithole's claims to the leadership of Zanu, regarding Mugabe as a usurper.

THE AFRICAN NATIONAL COUNCIL (ANC): THE RISE AND FALL AND RISE OF THE BISHOP

Abel Muzorewa, a 51 year-old Methodist Bishop, was confirmed as chairman of the ANC on 9 December 1974 in recognition of his position as a 'neutral' political figure and so best suited to head an umbrella organization intended to unite the three Zimbabwe nationalist factions. These were:

1. The Zimbabwe African People's Union (Zapu), formed in 1961, with Joshua Nkomo as its leader. The political leader of Zapu's military wing was Jason Moyo, assassinated in Lusaka in January 1977.

2. The Zimbabwe African National Union (Zanu) was formed in 1963 as a breakaway from Zapu. When its two principal leaders, Ndabaningi Sithole and Robert Mugabe, fell out while still in prison, two separate factions developed inside Zanu. Entirely different reasons led to a split in Zanu's military camp where violent rivalries developed between two Shona clans—the Nyika (or Manyika) and the Karanga.

3. The Front for the Liberation of Zimbabwe (Frolizi), formed initially by a group of young militants who had lost faith in both Zanu and Zapu, was subsequently taken over by two of Nkomo's exile leaders, Robert Chikerema (cousin to Mugabe) and George Nyandoro, who had broken with him.

The ANC had its origins in a remarkable movement which grew up rapidly in 1971-2 to fill the vacuum left when the Smith regime proscribed Zanu and Zapu after UDI. The trigger for this movement was the impending arrival of the Pearce Commission to test African opinion on the acceptability of proposals for independence negotiated between Salisbury and London.[29] Bishop Muzorewa, widely regarded at the time as the caretaker for Nkomo, emerged as its natural leader: his neutrality and political respectability guaranteed by his 'gaiters'. Until the ANC's recognition by the FLPs, the Bishop had shown no personal political ambition. Since Mugabe refused to have anything to do with the ANC and Nkomo remained aloof, the ANC-in-exile passed effectively into the hands of the Bishop, Sithole and Chikerema.

In 1975 and 1976 the Zimbabwe leaders had two constituencies—the cadres in the military camps in Tanzania and Zambia, and their electorate at home. Nkomo chose to work at home, leaving Jason Moyo to look after the Zapu camps. Mugabe concentrated all his efforts on the cadres in Mozambique. The Bishop elected to spend most of his time outside Rhodesia and Sithole, who faced prison if he returned, remained in exile.

Despite the FLPs' official endorsement, the ANC leadership failed to take control of the military camps. They blamed their failure on Tanzania and Mozambique for allegedly hindering their access to the camps. The truth is that they were not welcome there for reasons explained below. In fact, the ANC leaders made only two visits to the military camps in Tanzania in 1975, and none at all to those in Mozambique. However, in April they did go to Nachingwea, while it was still being evacuated by Frelimo forces to make way for a new Zimbabwe training camp.[30] In July, they were taken virtually under escort to an ANC camp near Iringa in Tanzania's central highlands. There they were bitterly criticized by the guerrillas for their continual feuding; allegations were also made that they had virtually abandoned the guerrillas in north-eastern Rhodesia, and had failed to organize supplies and equipment for the men in the camps. The ANC's fragile unity cracked in September 1975 when Sithole decided to form the Zimbabwe Liberation Council (ZLC) in an attempt to re-establish his control over Zanu against the increasingly successful challenge from Mugabe. By November 1975, when the FLPs withdrew their recognition from the political leaders, the Bishop had little visible support among the fighting cadres; two of his principal allies in exile were the two Frolizi leaders, Chikerema and Nyandoro. His political fortunes were at a low ebb when he finally decided—with the approach of the Geneva conference—to end his 15 months' self-exile on 3 October 1976. In Salisbury a crowd estimated at 100,000 welcomed 'the return of the messiah'. There could then be little doubt that he remained a popular figure in the home constituency. On the day before his return, Muzorewa had met Nkomo in Gaborone, the capital of Botswana; the general assumption was that they would form a political alliance. Nkomo certainly wanted an agreement with Muzorewa, but the Bishop was cool—possibly too many of his supporters were personally hostile to Nkomo; certainly they would not accept him as the leader in place of Muzorewa, and Nkomo was never disposed to playing second fiddle. But Mugabe chose Nkomo as his partner in the Patriotic Front, leaving the ANC without much military muscle. The Bishop led his own ANC team to the Geneva talks where his main tactical differences with the Patriotic Front led to the re-emergence of two hostile camps in the Zimbabwe liberation movement, but with the ANC having little support among the military leaders.

On his return home from Geneva on 11 December, Muzorewa was met by another massive turn-out of supporters chanting their distinctive catch-phrase 'Hea-vy'. But he suffered a slight setback when 12 leading supporters, including the Revd Canaan Banana and Nolan Makombe, switched their support to Mugabe. The worst blow came in November 1976 with the FLPs' decision to back only the Patriotic Front. The Bishop angrily accused the FLPs of trying to impose their own leadership on the Zimbabweans, and alleged a Zambian 'plot' to impose Nkomo as 'leader of Zimbabwe'—the Front-line States, he said, 'wittingly or unwittingly, were being used as a cover' with Mugabe 'a mere pawn'. He spoke scathingly of President Kaunda's 'unbeatable record of having backed losing horses'. Later, he even accused the FLPs of being in conspiracy with the 'imperialist powers' (including Britain) and the multi-national Lonrho to install Nkomo as Zimbabwe's first Prime Minister. He demanded a national referendum to allow black Rhodesians to choose their own leaders. As a result of these extraordinary allegations, the Bishop was declared *persona non grata* in Zambia, Tanzania and Mozambique. In January 1977, the OAU Council of Ministers endorsed the FLPs' decision to recognize only the Patriotic Front, robbing Muzorewa of most of his external African support. He still commands considerable support at home—but how much that will be worth if the country's future is to be decided on the battlefield rather than at the polls remains a question mark for the future.

THE ZIMBABWE AFRICAN NATIONAL UNION (ZANU): (1) THE ECLIPSE OF SITHOLE

The loneliest figure at the Geneva conference was Ndabaningi Sithole. Yet, just two years earlier, when he was freed from a Rhodesian prison—where he was serving a six-year sentence for plotting to assassinate Ian Smith—he was widely regarded as *the* leader of Zimbabwe's militants. But his downfall had begun in prison where an important group of Zanu executive members, led by Mugabe, had resolved to depose him because of allegations that he was in secret communication with the Smith regime. Nevertheless his reputation stood so high at the time of his release that the FLPs rejected Mugabe's allegations without even troubling to investigate them. Sithole's misfortunes were not entirely of Mugabe's making. They stemmed mainly from the bloody internicine quarrels in the Zanu camps in 1973 and 1974 which had culminated in the assassination of Herbert Chitepo on 18 March 1975.[31] Sithole (whose father was a Ndau, a small Shona clan in the east, and his mother Ndebeli) gave his own detailed version of what had happened in an Open Letter dated 10 May 1976:[32] 'The main theme of my letter is that Zanu, as we had first formed it, became [so] constantly subjected to a process of tribalization or regionalization that it completely lost the national perspective, with the result that unprecedented kidnappings and killings within Zanu took place and culminated in the assassination of Zimbabwe's greatly esteemed and admired Herbert Chitepo, who was regarded as a man of great national stature by all Zimbabweans who knew him.' He proceeded to show how 'tribalism or regionalism' had become a consuming element in the affairs of DARE (a Shona word), to whom Zanu's Central Committee had delegated its power in c. 1967 to prosecute the armed struggle. At its full strength in April 1969, all of DARE's eight leaders came from three Shona clans: three were Manyika (Easterners), three Zezuru (North-easterners), and two Karanga (South-easterners). There were no Matabele or members from other tribes. By 1975—after a bloody fight in the Nhari military camp in December 1974—DARE's composition was five Karanga and one Manyika. The Zezuru had been eliminated altogether, and the Karanga were dominant. 'For all practical purposes DARE had become nearly tribalized or regionalized,' Sithole commented. 'It therefore had ceased to represent Zanu as we knew it and had come to represent, in effect, Zatu (Zimbabwe African Tribal Union) or Zaru (Zimbabwe African Regional Union).' He claims that the new Military High Command was formed in November 1975 without proper consultation with the ANC, and that it was 'a continuation of the new and foreign thesis that the gun commands the Party . . . National leadership through the barrel of the gun is anathema to the people of Zimbabwe.' The notions of tribalism or regionalism did not originate with the people at home but with those in exile. He warned: 'The problem which we now face as a new nation is essentially a tribal or regional one.'

Sithole's opponents in Zanu offer a different interpretation of the violence in their military ranks.[33] They claim that Zanu's structure allowed for the removal of leaders by the rank and file at their biennial elections; this process was facilitated by Chitepo's 'democratic style of leadership', and in September 1975 had produced a break between the old conservative Zanu leaders and the young radical commanders. It was at this time that Sithole announced the formation of the Zimbabwe Liberation Council (ZLC) which attempted to entrench the Zanu 'rebels' such as Mukono, Mutambenengwe, Masangomai, Parirewa and Santana. These reactionaries were unacceptable to the Zanu rank and file, and to all Zanla (Zimbabwe African National Liberation Army) commanders as they were held responsible for the attempted coup in November 1974 and for the massacre of 59 Zanla guerrillas. The breach was further widened by Sithole's refusal to protest against the Zambian shooting of 11 Zanla guerrillas in a Zambian 'concentration camp' at Mboroma on 11 September 1975. Once the clash between the conservatives and the young radical commanders had occurred, the latter decided to ignore Sithole's orders to rely on negotiations and to refrain from full-scale guerrilla war. The Zanla commanders immediately requested support from the Mozambique and Tanzania governments. By November 1975, they had gained this support and formed the 18-man Military High Command in collaboration with Zapu commanders.

Sithole's decision to form the ZLC isolated him not only from the ANC but also from Zipa's newly-formed High Command. On 6 October 1976 [34] he insisted that whatever Mugabe or anybody else had said, 'I am the boss'. But it was a claim he has so far failed to justify. Dogged by ill-health and by his failure to rally the young cadres to his side, by 1977 Sithole appeared to be only a shadow of the once formidable nationalist leader.

THE ZIMBABWE AFRICAN NATIONAL UNION: (2) THE EMERGENCE OF ROBERT MUGABE

Robert Gabriel Mugabe (49) came into international prominence for the first time by his commanding presence at the Geneva conference. However he has in fact been a powerful force in Rhodesian politics since his return from Nkrumah's Ghana in 1960, where he had been a teacher and a keen student of the newly-emerging pattern of African politics. He immediately began to oppose Nkomo's leadership and assisted Sithole to set up Zanu as a rival to Zapu. But by the time he reached Geneva, his alliances were reversed. Mugabe's alliance with Nkomo is tactical. 'It is possible', he explained, 'to enter into an agreement with your political opponents to fight your enemy; but it is never possible to ally yourself with the enemy to fight your political opponents'.[35] The implication is clear: his alliance with Nkomo—his political opponent—is necessary to destroy Smith; but after the enemy's defeat he will feel free to engage in a further struggle for political power.

Mugabe is a survivor. He spent 10 years (1964-74) in Smith's prisons, passing three law exams and spending the rest of his time teaching young prisoners. On his release he refused to join the ANC or to accept any policy other than the supremacy of the armed struggle. He was defiantly rude to Kaunda and openly described him as an 'enemy' of the Zimbabwe struggle. His decision to take to the bush in Mozambique coincided with the mass exodus of volunteers and refugees across the border so that he found himself ideally situated to take the lead in organizing the new camps that had to be hastily built.

If Sithole's explanation of the tribal/regional conflicts within Zanu's military leadership is correct, it is odd that the Karanga-dominated command should have favoured Mugabe, a Zezuru clansman. Over-simplification of clan or tribal rivalries is clearly something to be avoided, more especially when one sees how many Zezuru are prominent in both ANC and Zapu councils, e.g. Chikerema in ANC (Frolizi); the Revd Henry Kachidza and two other members on the ANC Central Committee, and Willie Masuriwa in Zapu. (A breakdown of the ANC Central Committee in 1975 showed that it comprised five Nyikas, including the Bishop, no fewer than 10 Ndebele, three Zezuru, one Shangaan and one Karanga.)

The most likely explanation for Mugabe's support in the ranks of Zipa was that he, more than any of the other known political figures, accurately reflected the mood in the camps in 1975-6. As a militant intellectual with considerable political experience he was able to articulate the new spirit of the younger cadres with their strong desire to turn their backs on the past years of political quarrelling, unproductive negotiations and mass disillusion: for them, as for Mugabe, victory lay clearly and simply in the armed struggle.

Why, then, did Mugabe (with Zipa's support) go to Geneva? It was not because he thought the Geneva talks would succeed, but because they provided an important opportunity to stamp Zipa's (and his own) leadership on the independence movement. Moreover, on this occasion, Mugabe did not wish to antagonize the FLPs—and especially not Machel who was fully behind the Geneva initiative.

Mugabe insists that he is a socialist, not a Marxist: 'What I am saying is that we are socialist and we shall derive from the socialist systems of Tanzania and Mozambique. One cannot get rid of all the aspects of free enterprise. Even Russia and China have their *petits bourgeois,* but in Zimbabwe none of the white exploiters will be allowed to keep an acre of their land. We will keep our relations open with all countries and will certainly not be aligned to either of the two power blocs. But ours will be a socialist system, for the people . . . Not an inch of land would remain in private ownership. All of it would be nationalized and the black majority will not give a penny in compensation to any of the white landowners.'[36] But in a subsequent statement made only a few months later on BBC television, Mugabe expressed a more moderate view about white ownership of land: 'Fifty per cent of the land in Rhodesia is in the hands of 250,000 whites. This is unjust and will be corrected. White farmers must be prepared to part with sections of their lands so that it can be fairly divided. They will be free to choose their country of citizenship. But, of course, certain people, including Ian Smith, who constituted the illegal regime, will have to answer for their crimes in open court.'[37]

What of Mugabe's future? This depends in the short term on whether the Patriotic Front will survive and whether it will yet come to be fully accepted as the political wing of Zipa. Given the fissiparous nature of Zimbabwean politics and the purely tactical nature of the Nkomo-Mugabe association, it would be unrealistic to accept the Front's future as being assured; even the FLPs might, yet again, reverse their stand on recognizing it exclusively. What is even trickier is to try and predict the future of Mugabe's relations with Zipa. Is the Karanga-Zezuru quarrel finally buried beneath the heap of Zanu corpses? The only Zezuru in the Joint Command is the top commander, Rex Nhongo (see below). When the new Zanu executive was chosen in late 1976 the top post of president was inexplicably left vacant. Mugabe was appointed as secretary-general. Most of the other top appointments were Karanga—K. Mudzi (assistant secretary-general and foreign representative), Josiah Tongogara (secretary of military affairs), and Henry Hamadziripi (military commissioner). The other two members are R. Gumbo and K. Kangai.

ZIMBABWE AFRICAN PEOPLE'S UNION (ZAPU): JOSHUA NKOMO—AN OLD STAR RISES AGAIN

Joshua Nkomo (now 60) has played many parts in a political career stretching over a quarter of a century, but never more skilfully than in 1976. He finally emerged from his negotiations with Smith not as a badly compromised and irrelevant politician, but as a serious challenger for Zimbabwe leadership; allied to the militant Mugabe, and with the backing of Machel, Neto and the Russians—as well as of some Western governments. Nkomo's long years in detention have not only filled out his massive physique, but also built up in him a confident authority which was previously lacking. He emerged less the 'jovial Josh' and more the militant Joshua: tough-minded, relentlessly ambitious, and less afraid of showing the kind of anger he must often have felt in the past. His natural tribal constituency (the Ndebele or Matabele, and Kalanga) is a small one, making up less than 20% of the population, while the number of Zapu cadres under arms is probably no more than one-tenth of those in the training camps. (Although Nkomo is generally regarded as being Ndebele he is, in fact, Kalanga, a subsidiary group in Matabeleland. The Kalanga are also a Shona clan, deriving from the Karanga who came sough in Mzilikasi's time. The Kalanga are predominant in Zapu's leadership and included such figures, apart from Nkomo, as George Silundika, Edward Ndhlovu and the late Jason Moyo.) Because Nkomo has always been a nationalist he can count on the support of at least some of the older generation of politicians in Mashonaland. Nkomo is firmly committed to majority rule, but beyond that is not trammelled in any way by ideologies. He has always been at pains to make clear that his opposition to white rule does not imply hostility to white Rhodesians. 'They look at the future,' he says 'and think the African leaders, particularly those of the liberation movements, would like to see whites wiped out. This is completely mistaken. No one is fighting against white people as white people. I have struggled almost 30 years to remove an evil, the separation of people by races. I could not at the end of it find myself applying what I am fighting against. We regard people as people, and white people

22

as people like ourselves, with the emphasis on the *people* not on the *white*. Those of our white friends who decided to make our country their home are just as much citizens as anyone else.'[38] Nkomo's general political attitudes suggest that he is more likely to be a Kenyatta than a Nyerere or a Kaunda. His backing by the Soviets simply reflects their interests in opposing Zanu because the latter receive their military support from the Chinese. Despite his Russian patronage, Nkomo is the African leader whom most white Rhodesians and Anglo-American businessmen would like to see win—unless it is Muzorewa. Nkomo's strategy of continuing negotiations with Smith when the others had despaired was something of a gamble: if he could have pulled off a viable agreement he would have put himself in a commanding position to take over the country's leadership. However he also kept open his option to retreat to the military struggle.

Jason Moyo was the crucial figure in this two-prong strategy. Like his leader, this 52-year old former Bulawayo carpenter had shown a remarkable capacity to survive the many crises in Zapu's military camps. He was the principal link between Nkomo and the Russians. His assassination in Lusaka in January 1977 remains an unexplained mystery. Although it was given out at the time that he was killed by a letter-bomb mailed from Botswana, the authorities there have thrown doubt on the accuracy of this account. The nationalists' explanation for the killing is that it was done by 'Smith's agents'. There are better reasons for supposing that the assassins were Zimbabwean exiles, perhaps interested in weakening Nkomo's links with the Patriotic Front or in undermining Nkomo himself.

THE PATRIOTIC FRONT: A MARRIAGE OF CONVENIENCE

Nkomo went straight from the failure of his meeting with Muzorewa in Botswana to talks with Mugabe in Maputo on 5 October 1976. The groundwork for their agreement had already been prepared by Jason Moyo. The birth of the Patriotic Front was announced in Dar es Salaam on 10 October with a flourish of revolutionary slogans but with nothing to suggest an agreed political programme. The first attempt to formulate the Front's policy was made from 14-17 January 1977 when Mugabe and Jason Moyo (acting for Nkomo) agreed in Maputo to establish a co-ordinating committee of ten members comprising Zanu and 'ANC Zimbabweans', i.e. Zapu. They laid down four basic objectives: 'to liquidate imperialism and colonialism and thereby overthrow the racist minority regime; to create a national democratic state of the people of Zimbabwe; to eliminate all forms of capitalist exploitation and thus create conditions for a full-scale social revolution; and to guarantee national peace, security, equal rights and happiness for all in a free Zimbabwe.'

The Front served its purpose admirably at the Geneva conference as a tactical alliance between Zanu and Zapu and, indirectly, with Zipa. If it survives, it could eliminate the danger of a future civil war between two rival liberation armies—a danger mentioned by Nkomo[39] when he gave his reasons for allying himself with Mugabe: 'We took this very difficult move to try to avoid a war which would tear apart what we have been struggling for, for all these years.' He elaborated on this in a later statement: 'We don't want fighting between Zapu and Zanu. We don't want our people to wage a war after finally getting the freedom they have strived to achieve for years.'[40]

Nkomo's attitude to the Front is as coldly realistic as Mugabe's: 'The only forces that matter in the solution to the present conflict are those that command fire-power', he said in Geneva,[41] and added that only the leaders of the three military forces—Zanu, Zapu and Smith—sitting down together, could stop young Rhodesians fighting each other.

THE ZIMBABWE INDEPENDENCE PEOPLE'S ARMY (ZIPA): THE GUERRILLAS' INTERNAL STRUGGLES

Zipa was formally launched in November 1975 in the hope of ending the longstanding, bitter divisions between the Zapu and Zanu guerrilla forces as well as healing the internicine quarrels within Zanu itself. Up to then more guerrillas had died fighting each other than in fighting their enemy. At one point in 1974, as many as 2,000 guerrillas were in detention in Zambia and Tanzania—1,550 were detained for a time after Herbert Chitepo's death in 1974. Virtually the entire Zanu High Command was in prison, facing charges of murdering Chitepo and 59 guerrilla cadres. The pressures to unify the Zimbabweans came principally from the FLPs, and the initiative was taken mainly by Nyerere and Machel working through Col Hashim Mbita, the leader of the OAU Liberation Committee. Having finally given up hope of uniting the political leadership, they feared that as the end of the struggle came closer, the last phase could be a civil war between two black armies—the fear referred to by Nkomo above. The military cadres were ripe for the FLPs' initiative.

In September 1975 Zanu's cadres in the Mgagao camp (Tanzania) took the initiative in denouncing all the old Zimbabwe leaders, except for Mugabe. Soon afterwards, Jason Moyo got Nkomo's approval to begin unity talks with Mugabe's men. One of the intermediaries, Simon Mzenda (a Zanu commander), made a secret visit to Kabwe (Zambia) in November to consult with the former Zanu commander-in-chief, Josiah Tongogara, who was awaiting trial for Chitepo's murder. Tongogara authorized him to go ahead; they drew up a list of the nine Zanu leaders who with nine Zapu leaders were to form the new Joint High Command. In the latter part of November the two sides conferred for three days in the Mozambique bush, in the presence of the OAU Liberation Committee's representatives where they drew up an agreement which was publicly released in Dar es Salaam at the end of November. On 24 January 1976, Tongogara and two of his fellow-detainees in Kabwe, R. Gumbo and K. Kangai, smuggled out a letter to Mugabe calling on him 'formally to take over the Party leadership'. Mugabe did not reply until 4 April when he accepted the offer. This meant he had the approval of the detained Zanu leaders as well as that of the free commanders.

To implement the 1975 agreement, the FLPs decided it was necessary to integrate the Zapu and Zanu cadres by putting them together in the same training camps—Mgagao, Kingolwira and Nachingwea. After training they would proceed to camps in Mozambique close to the fighting zones. All the cadres would be required to abandon their commitment to old political parties and to take an oath of allegiance to Zipa and its Military Command. However, this method of ending friction in the camps failed. In mid-April 1976 there was a serious shooting affray in Kingolwira between Zapu and Zanu cadres which began over a simple dispute about who should stand first in the food queue: those who had just come off duty or those who were about to go on. As a result, the Liberation Committee removed about 800 Zapu cadres to Mgagao. There was another internicine Zanu fight on 5-6 June when the second most senior of the Zezeru leaders, Zadzu, was among those killed, leaving Rex Nhongo as the only senior commander from that clan. After a further fight, in Mgagao, this time between Zanu and Zapu, the two groups again had to be put into separate camps. There was one more serious internicine battle in November 1976 when, according to one report,[42] 33 guerrillas were killed and 14 injured.

Despite these setbacks the unified structure of the Military Command remains intact. Its top leader is still Rex Nhongo (Zanu), a 29-year-old veteran of the bush who wears horn-rimmed glasses and looks like an elegant athlete. He rejects communism and every other label: 'We know what we are fighting for—justice and to free our country.'[43] The other major Zanu figures in the Command are Dzinashe

Machingura (Deputy Army Political Commissar), Elias Hondo (Director of Operations), James Nyikadzinashe (Deputy of Security and Intelligence), Webster Gwayuwe and Dr Tadiwira. The two top Zapu members are Alfred Mangena (Chief Army Political Commissar) and Clement Nunyanyi (Chief of Security and Intelligence.)

All the military training in the camps is directed by the Chinese, Tanzanians and Mozambicans. The Chinese have filled this role ever since the first Zanu cadres were formed in the middle 1960s. By contrast, Zapu's first intake of recruits were all trained in Russia; Alfred Mangena, the Chief Army Political Commissar, is one of the survivors.

It is easier to analyse the nature of Zipa's leadership than it is the attitudes of the rank-and-file cadres, either in terms of their ideological commitment or loyalties to particular leaders. Because the Zanu camps are controlled by leaders opposed to Sithole and Muzorewa, it is possible to impose their political discipline over the cadres, and to suppress support for rival leaders on the justifiable ground of unity. Volunteers from Rhodesia not wanted for the guerrilla forces, or for whom no training facilities are immediately available, are put into labour camps. Muzorewa's lieutenants claim that cadres loyal to ANC have been drafted to these labour camps; this has inhibited others in the fighting ranks from openly stating their support for the Bishop. Whatever the truth of these allegations, there can be no doubt about the heavy emphasis on ideology that now forms part of the cadres' training.

Zipa's analysis of the nature of the Zimbabwe struggle was explained by its Deputy Army Political Commissar, Dzinashe Machingura, in an interview with the Mozambican Information Agency in October 1976: 'Our society is essentially a colonial society, and, as such, we have to launch a national democratic revolution to overthrow national oppression. This national democratic revolution will serve to reconcile the principal contradiction in Zimbabwe, which is characterized by the domination and oppression of the vast majority of the Zimbabwean people by a small minority racist reactionary clique of whites. From this we can say that all those who are opposed to the liberation and the independence of the Zimbabwean people are our enemies. These comprise the Smith racist regime and the imperialist powers that back him, puppet Africans serving the Smith regime and all those who are opposed to the independence of the Zimbabwean people. The target of the freedom fighters' bullets is the system of exploitation and the capitalistic enterprises and armed personnel which serve to perpetuate it.' Zipa's attitude was further elaborated in a statement broadcast in January 1977:[44] 'The racist part of the Rhodesia Front are trying to make the people of Zimbabwe believe that the present armed struggle is being waged in order to remove certain aspects of the oppressive and segregative social political system, while maintaining the overall system intact. They are trying to make the people of Zimbabwe believe that the liberation war is being prosecuted in order to reform the present social political system. This is a terrible misinterpretation of the Zimbabwean national liberation armed struggle . . . We are waging the national liberation armed struggle in Zimbabwe today in order to remove and destroy root, stem and branch—the present racist oppressive and reactionary economic system. In the words of the chairman of the Front-line Heads of State, President Julius Nyerere of Tanzania: "We have reaffirmed our support for the nationalist movements of Zimbabwe in their struggle to free Zimbabwe from colonialism and racist minority rule. The leaders of the Front-line States reiterated their conviction that the armed struggle is a product of colonialism, oppression and racism in Zimbabwe. This is a statement of fact. Therefore, the removal of these evils will create the conditions for peace and justice and inevitably bring to an end the armed struggle." Further, in our own words we are waging the current armed struggle in order: (1) to smash imperialism, colonialism and the racist regime in our country; (2) to eliminate all forms of capitalist exploitation and thus create conditions for a full-scale social revolution; (3) to create a national democratic state of the people of Zimbabwe; and (4) to guarantee national peace, security, equal rights and happiness for all in a free Zimbabwe. Our armed struggle is both a national and an ideological struggle . . . The people of Zimbabwe are demanding the complete, total and unconditional surrender of political and military power by the racists to the people themselves. Anything short of the total and complete removal and destruction of racism, colonialism and oppression will not do.'

THE DEFENDERS (1) THE RHODESIANS: WHO WILL STAY?

The war most white Rhodesians thought would never come finally hit them in 1976.[45] According to official estimates, there were 1,500 'terrorists' operating inside Rhodesia by the end of the year; another 2,000 fully trained cadres in base camps in Mozambique; and a further 2,000 still in training.[46] The African estimate of guerrilla volunteers immediately available is 20,000, with a limitless supply ready to come forward as the fighting develops. The Smith regime could put a total of 50,000 security forces in the field against them, but only by calling up every able-bodied white Rhodesian and using every black volunteer; this would stretch even further the already heavily strained economy. Of the total number, 6,000 are regulars; roughly half are white. The all-white Territorial Forces number 16,500; National Servicemen 1,200; the older Reservists c. 3,000; the regular Police Force 7,000 (two-thirds black), and the Police Reserves c. 12,000, mostly white. The Air Force has 12 Hawker Hunter fighters, 11 Canberra bombers, 24 Vampires and 16 Alouette helicopters. Defence spending has shot up from £34.8m in 1971-2 to £122m in 1976-7—a huge 34% increase over the previous year. Call-up was extended from 12 to 18 months. The economy was under siege with virtually no real growth; manufacturing was down by 7.1% in the first nine months of 1976; the value of retail sales dropped by 3.2%, the worst figure since 1965; and tourism had slumped. Defence spending became the second biggest item in the Budget after education. But the critical figure was emigration—the final test of confidence. In 1976, 7,076 white Rhodesians left permanently—1,158 in December alone. A second vital indicator was that between 2,000-3,000 reservists did not report for duty and over 1,000 young men called up for national service were reported missing.[47]

A new phrase came into vogue: 'chicken-run'. It was used to describe the exodus of the whites. 'The word "chicken" has now become just about the worst epithet that can be applied in Rhodesia'.[48] There were those who felt 'the sooner we see the last of the chickens, the better. Then we'll know that those who remain are the sort of people we want as fellow countrymen.'[49] But others asked: 'Why should I stay on? What sort of future is there for me? I don't want to get killed fighting for principles I'm not sure are correct'.[50] An 18-year old soldier who had escaped from the army simply felt: 'I'm too young to want to die in a war that can't be won, and, anyway, I don't want to live under black rule'.[51] But a large number, like Kenneth Street aged 65, were unhappy about the future but couldn't decide to leave: 'Kenya had been good to us and Zambia had been good too. But we were just fed up with being kicked around. I don't know what the Africans had against us. Perhaps it was that we were snobs. We were rather enamoured of what Mr Smith was saying and admired his stand. Everything about Rhodesia appealed to us. People coming out from Britain expected a certain kind of life—and Rhodesia seemed to promise it.

Now the whole thing is going to happen here again . . . We've all decided to stay and stick it out.'[52]

Whatever does happen in the end, it certainly will not be the 'way of life' which UDI was supposed to preserve; the only question for most white Rhodesians is whether the future will offer enough to make staying worthwhile. How long will it take to find out? These are the questions in 1976 over which white Rhodesians have begun to agonize seriously for the first time. It is by no means certain how many 'real' white Rhodesians there are. The figure usually quoted is c. 270,000, which is almost certainly too high—even taking into account the 10,000 to 20,000 Portuguese from Mozambique and Angola who were quietly admitted. If one subtracts the number of fairly recent British immigrants, who only went for 'the good life', and the South Africans, who have no final commitment to stay, certainly not under black rule, it is doubtful whether the permanent white population is as high as 180,000.

The mood of white Rhodesians shifted between hope and despair in 1976-7. The welcome given to Smith's announcement of his settlement terms with Kissinger in September 1976 showed how anxious the great majority was for a quick political settlement—even if it meant black rule. Only a tiny extremist minority group supported those who had placed a wreath of white carnations on the base of Cecil Rhodes' statue with a card that read: 'In memory of independent white Rhodesia. Born 11 November 1965. Died 24 September 1976. Murdered by abandoned Rhodesian Front principles.' Yet, when Smith turned his back on Geneva and rejected the British proposals in January 1977, there was no significant protest among whites. Why not? When Smith announced his settlement terms in September 1976 he laid special stress on the provision that defence and security would remain in white Rhodesian hands during the transition; the impression he deliberately created was that negotiations for a black majority government would be with 'moderate Africans—chaps like Josh Nkomo'—not with the 'Marxist terrorists' like Mugabe. But the evidence of Geneva was that a settlement was possible only with leaders acceptable to the guerrillas; and now Nkomo was among them, along with Mugabe. Moreover, there could be no question of either the Ministries of Law and Order and Defence remaining in the hands of the Smith regime during the transition; the best that might be hoped for was that they would be held by Whitehall—and this was almost as much of an anathema to the Rhodesia Front leaders as are the guerrillas. There were two other developments which helped to shift white Rhodesian thinking after the euphoria of September 1976. One was the ease with which their troops had crossed into Mozambique on three occasions since November and inflicted heavy punishment on the guerrillas; the other was the new divisions between the Patriotic Front and Bishop Muzorewa's ANC, and the evidence of the Bishop's popular support at home. What now began to seem possible was 'a deal' with the 'moderates'—now led by the Bishop instead of Nkomo; and the likelihood of being able to stop the guerrillas. No less important was the growing belief that Smith might be right after all: if only they could hold out long enough, SA and the US would change their position and come to the defence of a new 'majority-ruled' Rhodesia.

THE DEFENDERS (2) WHERE WILL SOUTH AFRICA STAND?

'Thoughtful South Africans have ever since 1965 asked, with mounting urgency, what Salisbury was going to do about it (sharing freedom within a common society); unhappily without getting answers which fitted the times. So the message became more insistent: "You are in a fix, involving us, which is bound to

get worse. You profess to have a policy for, in effect, decolonizing and emancipating your black peoples. We have little faith in it, either for you or for ourselves, because it may well end up in black tribal war and domination; but if you do believe in it, surely now is the time to implement it with all deliberate speed." '—Piet Cillie, Editor of Die Burger, *Capetown.*[53]

South Africa's leaders shared many of the fears felt by white Rhodesians, but few of their illusions. Ever since the collapse of the Portuguese in 1974, Prime Minister John Vorster has made no secret of his view that the only policy for his northern neighbour was to accept the inevitability of majority rule and to achieve it quickly through a peaceful settlement since the alternative was 'too ghastly to contemplate'. The spectre that haunted Vorster was of communism advancing down the continent, behind the 'forces of black violence', right up to SA's borders. If that day ever came the apartheid Republic would be isolated and exposed to two major risks: incipient black violence exploding inside the Republic, and withdrawal of Western support because of larger national interests. There was no lack of evidence in 1976 to support both these probabilities. The sea-change in American policy announced by Kissinger in Lusaka in April had shown how sensitive the Western nations were to the shifting balance of power in the region; and the urban violence in Soweto and Capetown from September to December demonstrated the dangerous mood of black South Africans.[54] For Vorster there was thus everything to be gained from an early and peaceful settlement of his 'two border problems'—Rhodesia and Namibia—which could help defuse the growing mood of violence in the sub-continent, reduce the opportunities for Communist involvement, and (so Vorster believed) buy more time to show that his own solvent for the race problems of SA—Separate Development and independent Homelands—could work. 'Buying time' therefore became a vital determinant of SA foreign policy. This made Vorster a willing ally of any party ready to negotiate a settlement in Rhodesia; it was the pursuit of this policy that first brought him into close contact with the FLPs in his search for detente in 1974-5.[55] When those contacts were broken off because of his miscalculated military intervention in Angola in 1975,[56] Vorster responded eagerly to Kissinger's offer to try to bridge the gap between the leaders of black-ruled and white-ruled southern Africa. However, Vorster was not entirely free to play his strong hand in Rhodesia both for fear of possible reactions from his own (white) electorate, and because SA cannot co-operate in the application of sanctions to achieve political change.

These factors require elaboration. First, since effective legal political power is exclusive to the white electorate, the ruling party's parliamentary caucus of Afrikaner MPs must reflect their interests, wishes and fears. The most crucial of their interests is to defend White Supremacy; the task of persuading MPs to accept any policy which could possibly be thought to weaken the *status quo* is a formidable one which has already defeated two of the country's most powerful Prime Ministers. Both General J. C. Smuts and Dr H. F. Verwoerd were thwarted in their attempts to make the kind of radical changes each felt to be necessary to secure the 'white man's future' at the southern tip of the continent. Despite Vorster's commanding authority, his position is by no means unassailable. He has failed to carry his white electorate with him on a number of major changes, especially those affecting the black urban population which the Government itself believes are urgently necessary. Even in the relatively harmless area of sport, Vorster has failed. Despite his own acceptance of the need for integrated club teams, in order to end SA's isolation in international sport, he has failed to muster the necessary support in Parliament to change the law.[57] Nevertheless, he did gather sufficient backing for his policy of accepting rapid majority rule in both Rhodesia and Namibia. He could sell these changes to his electorate as the price for bolstering up their own security; moreover, the two populations concerned are outside the Republic. Even so, both these decisions upset influential groups of the so-called *verkramptes* ('inward-looking people') in his caucus, and this makes it important for him to avoid any false step that could strengthen their position and bring him down. It is a moot point whether Vorster could have been more courageous than he was, both over Rhodesia and at home after the warning of Soweto. However, he was inclined to caution, especially after the failure of his military intervention in Angola. He believes, rightly or wrongly, that his white electorate will back his Rhodesian policy only so long as he is not actually seen to be pressuring the white Rhodesians. This means that every time he leans on Smith he disguises it by vigorously repudiating any such intention.

The second constraint on Vorster's Rhodesian policy arises from the need to avoid co-operating in anything smacking of economic sanctions or blockade, since these are the weapons which the international community has been urged over many years to apply against SA itself to make it abandon apartheid. If white Rhodesia were in the end to be brought down by a blockade, assisted by SA, the case for applying this kind of pressure against the Republic would be strengthened. So, while Vorster has impeded the traffic of Rhodesian goods on the SA railways and harbours system (on the justifiable grounds that his railways and ports are overstrained) he is constrained by these longer-term considerations from closing the border with Rhodesia. Thus, while Vorster sees it as vital to SA's national interest to help produce majority rule in Rhodesia by peaceful negotiations, he is inhibited from taking the two simple measures that would make it impossible for the Smith regime to hold out for five minutes: cutting off their fuel supplies which originate entirely in SA; and stopping the supply of weapons from the Republic's factories. The second measure could, in fact, be taken without closing the border; but it could not be done in secret. Smith would announce to the world that Vorster was preventing white Rhodesians from defending their lives against 'murderous terrorists'. The white blacklash in SA is easy to imagine and Mr Smith is adept at using it against Vorster. At the same time, Vorster is also acutely embarrassed by any publicity given to the supply of SA weapons to the Rhodesian army. This was shown in November 1975 when Smith told the US publisher William Randolph Hearst: 'At present we are getting enough arms from SA to keep us going'.[58] Although the interview with Hearst was in the presence of two of his staff, Smith on the very next day publicly denied that he had said anything about arms from SA: the lines from Pretoria had been sizzling overnight.

So, while it is obvious what steps Vorster might himself take to avoid the 'ghastly alternative' he fears, it is politically understandable that he has not so far gone for the 'quick kill'. He is trapped by circumstances. It is a dangerous predicament, and not just confined to Rhodesia: it applies equally to the internal affairs of the Republic. At a time when SA is passing through the most critical period of its modern history, its Prime Minister is paralyzed by indecision; he knows that urgent changes must be made quickly especially to assuage the black urban discontent; but he is afraid to move because of the risk of losing white electoral support.[59] The dangers on his home front make it all the more important that diplomatic initiatives over Rhodesia and Namibia should succeed. Meanwhile, like the FLPs, he must prepare for the military alternative in case diplomacy should fail in the end.

International involvement in a war in Rhodesia would present SA with the difficult choice of deciding whether to intervene itself, or to keep its troops south of the Limpopo river. Whatever choice SA finally makes, the conflict seems almost certain to open up greater dangers on three other fronts. An upsurge in black urban violence is an inevitable result at home. The frontier with Mozambique, which abuts on two Homelands (KwaZulu and Kazangulu), offers the best terrain for the Russian-backed guerrilla forces of the African National Congress, whose leaders (together with those of the SA Communist Party), began to shift their operations to Maputo in 1976. But it is the Namibian front which is likely to test SA's defences most directly, since a military challenge there would certainly fully involve the SA army.

THE FOURTH FRONT: ANGOLA'S NEIGHBOUR NAMIBIA

As events unfolded in 1976 and early 1977, Namibia's immediate future became more directly interlinked with the outcome of the Rhodesian negotiations. This was inevitable for several reasons. The FLPs' *Strategy for Southern Africa's Liberation* (adopted by the OAU in 1975)[60] linked the two territories as immediate targets for independence. The outcome of the Angolan struggle in 1975 had left SA more vulnerable to the guerrilla forces of the South West African People's Organization of Namibia (Swapo) from across the Cunene river. Swapo had acquired a militant ally in President Agostinho Neto's MPLA regime—as well as a new, independent base-country from which to operate, instead of having to rely on the more remote and less satisfactory camps in Zambia. No less important to Swapo was the military presence of the Russians and Cubans in Angola; by their very presence they imposed a threat to SA, and so increased the pressures on Vorster to find a settlement for this 30-year old international dispute between the UN and SA over the future of the former mandated territory. At the same time, they offered the hitherto carefully non-aligned Swapo leadership a new option for military support should they need it.[61]

Although Kissinger's diplomatic initiative put the main emphasis on Rhodesia it also included Namibia; and the FLPs gave equal priority to both. The British Government took an independent initiative by sending a Foreign Office envoy, Martin Reith, to Namibia in September 1975 to test the chances of arranging a Geneva-type conference. Kissinger persuaded Vorster to accept the idea for such a conference in their talks at Zurich (see below). The problem was to agree about who would be invited. Swapo insisted that the black side of the negotiators should be restricted to themselves and their own nominees, with the SA Government forming the other side. Despite its support for the UN stand that SA is in illegal occupation of Namibia—Swapo believes that nothing practical can be achieved except through direct negotiations with the SA Government. Vorster—who describes Swapo as 'a gang of communists', and who has an undisguised loathing for their burly, bearded leader, Sam Nujomo—simply refused to consider any conference which included Swapo at all, let alone as sole representatives of the blacks. Vorster believed also that there should be no official role for SA at such a conference; he insisted that it was now the affair only of the Namibians. Nevertheless, he undertook not to stand in the way of a meeting between the members of the 'Turnhalle' conference and Swapo. Turnhalle is the old German hall in Windhoek where 135 white and black Namibians have been engaged since 1975 in working out an independence constitution for the territory[62] in fulfilment of a SA pledge to the UN to arrange for Namibia's freedom before the end of 1978. Swapo boycotted the conference for two main reasons: it was held under South African rather than UN auspices; and its representatives were selected on an ethnic basis which excluded the political movements.

The task of diplomacy was to arrange 'a table' which would overcome (1) SA's objections to sitting down with Swapo and, indeed, to attending a conference at all;

(2) Swapo's objections to sitting down with the Turnhalle members as an independent delegation; and (3) Swapo's insistence on being recognized as the exclusive spokesman for black Namibians. While Kissinger made some progress in 'arranging the table', the diplomatic initiative faltered after the failure of the Geneva conference on Rhodesia. Vorster urged the Turnhall delegates to speed up their work to produce a constitution. The clear implication was that he was in a hurry to declare the territory independent, just as the independence of the Transkei was presented as a *fait accompli* to the international community.[63] If any attack were then launched against Namibia it would be against an 'independent State' with a majority black government, which would be free to 'invite in' the SA army to assist them to defend their independence. Another advantage to SA from such an arrangement would be that the anti-Swapo black Namibians would have a vested interest of their own to defend—so SA would effectively be dividing the black ranks. Swapo was by no means alone in denouncing Vorster's plan: the UN, the OAU, the Non-Aligned Nations' Summit, the European Economic Community, the Commonwealth and the US all insisted that Swapo's full involvement in the negotiations for independence was an essential pre-requisite to international recognition of a free Namibia.

While Vorster was urging speed on the Turnhalle conference, Swapo was busy regrouping itself in southern Angola, preparatory to launching a major guerrilla campaign inside Namibia. Its leadership was not agreed about taking up the Russian option (which would have involved 'phasing out' the Chinese military instructors from their camps); but they were getting more Russian and Chinese arms. In September 1975 the OAU Liberation Committee also began flying arms into Swapo's camps in Angola from Dar es Salaam. This arms flow, taken on the initiative of the FLPs, could be interpreted as a move to reduce the pressures on Swapo to take up the Russian option. However, as only the Russians and Cubans are in a position to give Swapo the kind of military support they would need if it came to a major conflict with the massive concentration of SA troops that were congregating south of the Cunene River and in the Caprivi Strip, the chances of Swapo invoking the Moscow factor remain high. Yet Vorster, who fears nothing more than an extension of Russian influence along his borders, gave all the appearances of being ready to ignore this risk rather than to negotiate with a movement which, in the past, has looked more to the West than to the East for its political and moral, if not its military support; and to the Chinese rather than the Russians for the arms which no Western country was prepared to provide.

There are three probable reasons for Vorster's contradictory policies on Namibia. The first is that he genuinely believes that if Swapo were to form the government in Namibia it would be tantamount to letting in 'the communists'—so fixed is his idea about Swapo's true nature. The second reason is that he has already gone too far in his commitment to the black Namibian leaders engaged in the Turnhalle talks, such as Chief Clemens Kapuuo and the Ovambo tribal leaders, to risk their future. (Yet this can only be a partial explanation since Kapuuo and all the other Turnhalle delegates, including the whites, told the British envoy, Martin Reith, that they were willing to sit down with Swapo.) The third reason is that if Rhodesia goes up in flames, Vorster could not afford to withdraw his army from their forward positions in Namibia. By the same token if negotiations over Rhodesia prove successful, he would have less to fear from coming to an arrangement with Swapo. Successful Rhodesian negotiations were therefore also seen as the key to successful negotiations over Namibia.

THE INTERLOCUTOR: DR KISSINGER'S DIPLOMACY

At the beginning of 1976 the US Secretary of State's career had begun to look distinctly frayed. After Watergate and the CIA investigations had come the defeat in Congress of his proposals to counter the Russian/Cuban military intervention in Angola. For Kissinger, Angola was a personal debacle; for southern Africa it had opened up an entirely new scenario with the prospect of escalated guerrilla wars, the rise of more revolutionary-minded movements, heavier pressures on the more 'moderate' African governments, a shortened time-fuse for the survival of the apartheid Republic, and the real possibility of a greater Soviet role in the sub-continent. African leaders and movements who had looked to Washington for support over Angola had been badly let down; they would be less likely to rely on Western sources in future. Among Western leaders—most of whom had 'looked the other way' in order to avoid getting involved in Angola—only Henry Kissinger seemed to have the imagination needed to try to do something to rescue the situation—and, perhaps, to restore some of the dazzle to his reputation.

Kissinger had given very little of his mind to black Africa until the Angolan affair; his only major decision in this area was to choose the wrong option from a number offered in the National Security Council Memorandum 39 of 1970.[64] The one he chose—to tilt the balance of US policy towards the white regimes of southern Africa—fitted in with Nixon's ideas and with those of his subsequently discredited lobbyists.[65] But it turned out to be disastrously wrong, resting chiefly on the premise that the black guerrilla movements would fail in the Portuguese colonies. This error weakened American influence in the area at a crucial time, but without strengthening the White Redoubt. Angola became the tombstone on the grave of NSCM 39.

When Kissinger finally turned his mind seriously to the problems of the sub-continent he quickly came to four broad conclusions. First, that the balance had to be tilted the other way—towards support for majority rule. Second, that no initiative on his part could succeed without the co-operation of the FLPs and, especially of its chairman, Nyerere. Third, that the SA Prime Minister was the key factor; and fourth, that close Anglo-American co-operation was important. Having made up his mind about what should be done, Kissinger began to send out signals that if his services were wanted, he was ready to undertake a diplomatic initiative in Africa.

The connection with Nyerere came about almost by accident. One morning, a Tanzanian official listening to the 'Voice of America' was surprised to hear that Kissinger was contemplating a visit to Africa. His inquiry to the US Embassy in Dar es Salaam confirmed its accuracy. When he passed the message on to State House, Nyerere's response was not only positive but enthusiastic. Only President Machel among the FLPs was at first unsure about welcoming an American initiative. Nyerere is said to have given him the reply which he was later to repeat to those who found it hard to understand why he should have been willing to accept Kissinger's intervention: 'We want the two greatest sources of power on our side—God and Kissinger'. Coming from a true Believer, this reply was not just a clever jest: it reflects Nyerere's understanding of power. While he has written of his fear of the abuse of power (even of his own) he has never been afraid to use it positively. Kissinger, he felt, should be given the chance to prove that he seriously meant to help promote majority rule in southern Africa—even if it upset the Russians and Cubans (see below).

Kissinger's African diplomacy was significantly different from the highly personalized style and squirrelish habit of hiding his strategy deep inside his breast pocket which had characterized his Middle East shuttles. On this occasion he assumed the role of the super-salesman with three major clients—Britain, Vorster and the FLPs—each of them suspicious of him and of each other. He was not going to try to supplant the British by taking over their responsibilities for Rhodesia (which, anyway, would not suit the American mood), but to promote the settlement terms offered in Callaghan's 22 March proposals. And if he succeeded, to stand aside and allow the British to carry on, having used to good effect the US 'muscle' which was lacking in the British negotiating position. To the FLPs and Vorster, Kissinger offered himself as an interlocutor. This was his own description of his role: he saw himself as bridging the gap that had opened between black and white leaders when their contacts were broken off after the Angolan episode. He could discover what each side wanted, how far they were able and prepared to go, and to clarify misunderstandings. This role was quite different from that of a mediator. Kissinger's aides have described how he worked once he became convinced of the importance of Africa.[66] 'He wants to know everything he can and to meet the various leaders and establish as intimate a relationship as possible to convince them of his even-handedness and sympathy. This requires considerable exchanges of messages, confidentiality and constant travel. He then begins what is regarded by his aides as the most difficult stage: analyzing the positions with all sides and persuading each one, even in the first stage of negotiation, to temper its demands and understand the problems of the others. When the initial proposals and counter-proposals are submitted through Kissinger, he passes them on but inevitably comments on them, telling each side that he knows that a particular demand would be completely unacceptable, but suggesting that if it was modified somewhat it might be acceptable. Meanwhile he and his aides draw up a synthesis of the two positions and offer discreet compromise solutions.' Kissinger stuck rigorously to this role of go-between rather than of mediator except on one occasion—when he met Smith in Pretoria; that single deviation fatally flawed his otherwise impeccable diplomacy.

If the Secretary's sophisticated diplomatic operation succeeded, the US would clearly benefit. Not only would the US (and Kissinger personally) retrieve some of the prestige lost over the blunders of Angola, but by preventing the spread of violence they could hope to choke off the risks of the Russians repeating their Angolan victory in a vital area—and, perhaps, even repeat their Middle Eastern success of throwing the Soviets heavily back on the defensive. All this could be achieved without destroying the claim that the US was serving the cause of world peace by, to quote Kissinger, 'heading off a race war in southern Africa'.

Kissinger saw the first crucial hurdle as winning the support and trust of Nyerere, whom he met for the first time in late April 1976. For their first informal get-together, Nyerere invited Kissinger to dinner at his beach house at Masisini, just outside the capital. Kissinger was naturally anxious to make a good impression; he was also tense (according to one of his aides) because of the strangeness of his surroundings. Having no previous experience of African intellectuals on their home ground, he did not know what to expect, and especially not from a host reputed to prefer Chinese to Americans. Nyerere was at his most quixotic: 'Ah, Mr Secretary,' he greeted his guest, 'I have a surprise for you'. At once he disappeared behind a screen in the reception room. Kissinger's entourage say they could feel the Secretary stiffen as Nyerere reappeared—leading a very ancient woman who came up close to him. Nyerere introduced her as his mother, down for a short visit from her native village of Butiama. Kissinger's relief was brief. The old lady delivered a rapid staccato of strange syllables in Ki-Zanakia tongue not understood even by most Tanzanians present. Before he could make any response, another rapid burst of words was directed at him. Nyerere was apparently much amused, Kissinger totally bemused. His mother, Nyerere finally announced, wanted him to translate what she had said. She wished to greet this distinguished visitor who had come half-way round the world to see her son. She had heard that he was famous in his own country—even a famous professor! She hoped he would not hesitate to point out to her son any mistakes he might make! The ice was broken. By the end of the visit both men felt that, whatever their reservations, they could respect each other.

Nyerere set out the minimum demands of the FLPs. Both saw Vorster as the key to the change in Rhodesia and Namibia. Nyerere felt Vorster had the power to do what was needed in Namibia, and could exercise the necessary pressure on Rhodesia; he impressed on Kissinger the importance of concentrating on Namibia, since he felt a quick breakthrough was possible on that front. He pointed out that while the FLPs were in a position to stop foreign intervention in Rhodesia because they controlled all the access routes, the situation was different in Namibia.

It was at his next stop, Lusaka, that Kissinger unfolded the Americans' new 'post-Angola' policy with its commitment to majority rule in SA, as well as in Rhodesia and Namibia.[67] 'What is unique (in SA),' he said, 'is the extent to which racial discrimination has been institutionalized, enshrined in laws and made all-pervasive'. His peroration, quoted earlier, caused Kaunda to embrace him publicly. It was a personal triumph, but this American 'wind of change' speech did nothing to dispel the war clouds. In the middle of May, Kaunda predicted that southern Africa would become the battleground in an ideological and strategic conflict between the superpowers;[68] the countries in the region would become pawns in the power game of nations whose aim is 'world hegemony'—a familiar Chinese phrase which he thrust at the Russians. This dark picture of the future had for long been Kenneth Kaunda's nightmare of what could go wrong. A few days later, President Machel left on a 'friendship visit' to Moscow. On 20 May the British High Commission in Lusaka, responding to a call made by Kaunda, urged all British passport-holders to leave Rhodesia for their own safety. Ten days later, Kaunda told American journalists that as soon as Zipa was ready a new war front would be opened up from Zambia. The only whites who would have a place in an independent Zimbabwe, he said, would be those who were themselves 'revolutionaries'. 'They are going to lose their farms, their industries. The people will take them over because this is a revolution now. I cannot see anything else than that. It is too late.' In July, when Nyerere spoke at the formal opening of the Tanzara Freedom railway, built by the Chinese, he declared: 'In Rhodesia the die is cast. The armed struggle is on. Only majority rule will bring that armed struggle to an end . . . In Namibia also the armed struggle has begun. It is not yet a full-scale war . . . We are determined that SA shall belong equally to every one of its citizens regardless of race. Do not let us be under any illusion about the implications of such a commitment.'

Against this darkening background of a sub-continent already engulfed in fighting, Kissinger made his first public move to tackle the 'key factor' in the situation. He met SA's Prime Minister in a small Bavarian village at the beginning of July. Almost nothing that passed between them was allowed to leak out, but clearly enough common ground emerged to encourage both to meet again, this time in Zurich for three days of talks from 3-6 September. Before setting out for Zurich, Kissinger went to Philadelphia on 31 August 'to talk about Africa—one of the compelling concerns of our time'. His speech—the first major statement on Africa he had ever made to an American audience—was important for showing how quickly Kissinger had attuned himself to the African wavelength. 'When we read of young African students killed in riots, of guerrilla raids, or refugee camps attacked in reprisal, the reality lies not in the cold statistics that the media report. In Africa, it is the death of men, women and children; it means hopes extinguished and dreams shattered. The grand issues of strategy or the complexity of negotiations are no consolation to innocent brutalized victims. As long as these conflicts fester, Africans of all races will be caught up in a widening and escalating cycle of violence. Until these wars are ended, Africa faces a future of danger, anguish and growing risks of foreign intervention . . . And in SA itself, the recent outbreaks of racial violence have underscored the inevitable instability of a system that institutionalized human inequality in a way repugnant to the world's conscience . . . I restated on African soil America's rejection of the principle and practice of apartheid. I called on SA to demonstrate its commitment to peace and harmony on the continent by facilitating early solutions in Rhodesia and Namibia . . . There is no better guarantee against foreign intervention than the determination of African nations to defend their own independence and unity . . . One fact is clear: a time of change has come again to Africa . . . What Africa needs now is not a return to the exploitive or interventionist practices of decades past. Nor does it need exuberant promises and vapid expressions of goodwill. It requires concrete commitments to progress—political and economic. It requires our readiness to co-operate as sovereign equals on the basis of mutual responsibility and mutual benefit.' Finally, he stated in advance the message he was proposing to take with him to his meeting with Vorster: '. . . the white population of Rhodesia and Namibia must recognize that majority rule is inevitable. The only issue is what form it will take and how it will come about . . .'

The Philadelphia speech had a predictably bad reception in SA, and especially with Vorster. Nevertheless, their Zurich encounter left Kissinger hopeful that enough had been achieved 'both in procedures and in substance' to justify his embarking on a second mission to Africa. Vorster, by contrast, doused all hopes of a settlement in Namibia by saying flatly that no member of his government would ever sit down with Swapo to talk about the territory's future.

THE KISSINGER SHUTTLE: 'GETTING OUT OF A BLOODY MESS'

'Time is running out. If we can't get negotiations started in Rhodesia by the end of the year, it will be a bloody mess. At issue is not only the future of two States in southern Africa, but the potential evolution of all Africa with its profound impact on Europe and on the Middle East.'—Dr Kissinger

The FLPs met in Dar es Salaam from 5-7 September 1976 to decide whether the confidential information brought to them by Kissinger's special envoy, following his meeting with Vorster in Zurich, offered enough to justify continuing support for the American diplomatic initiative. Now, for the first time, Angola's President Agostinho Neto, became a member of the club. Also, all the liberation movements in southern Africa were invited to present their views—another new procedure. The FLPs' final communique pledged them to 'further intensify the armed struggle in Zimbabwe', but it said nothing about Kissinger's future initiative. However, Nyerere was in fact authorized to inform Kissinger that they 'welcomed the idea' of his shuttle. It was not an invitation, just an assenting nod. The distinction is a subtle but important one—especially when the FLPs were carrying Neto along with them.

Kissinger left for Africa on 13 September in an attempt as he described it 'to head off a race war between blacks and whites'. For how many years had critics of the African policies of the US and other Western nations warned of just such a danger? No key figure in a position of power had been less willing to listen to the 'Africa bores' than Kissinger—until he came to realize, as he told Washington journalists on 11 September, that 'the risks to world peace are very severe. War has already started in southern Africa, and there is a grave danger of its expansion. Clearly, if outside powers become very active in southern Africa, the danger of that area becoming an arena for superpower conflicts becomes very great.' Having left it all so late, what more could the President of the US say with truth than that the mission had 'no assurance of success, but it is worth the risk in a continent vital to us all'. A striking editorial in the *Washington Post* (9 September 1976) put the risks in some perspective: 'One can fairly criticize the Administration for coming late to southern Africa and for coming there less out of concern for racial and human justice than out of a fear that the Soviet Union would exploit the larger regional turbulence as it did the struggle inside Angola. But the crisis in southern Africa is real and it threatens to rage out of control with almost unimaginable costs and consequences. For the US to play it safe and to do less than it could to avert a holocaust would not only be bad diplomacy, contributing to world disorder, it would be an abdication by the US of moral obligation and responsibility to the world community. During the years of US neglect of Africa, others have had plenty of time and room to defuse the situation, but nothing has been done.'

NOTES FROM KISSINGER'S CONVERSATIONS EN ROUTE TO EUROPE/AFRICA (13 SEPTEMBER)[69]

'Substantially Namibia is the easier problem, but procedurally the more difficult. Rhodesia is the other way round. It is easier to visualize a mechanism for Rhodesia. Vorster would not have gone this far if he did not want to make a major effort. He knows what the US needs in terms of concessions. We have to assume he is doing it in good faith. We have evidence that SA is putting the screws on Rhodesia. For example, the withdrawal of para-military police last year, the withdrawal of helicopter pilots manning the gunships, and the congestion of Rhodesian goods in the SA rail and port systems which appear to be contrived.' Kissinger said that Nyerere had agreed to some of the details of the US/UK perception of how things might work, but that he (Kissinger) was still afraid that if he failed to get a commitment from the whites the blacks might raise their demands. Kissinger's minimum hopes were a commitment from SA to work towards majority rule in Rhodesia on the basis of the US/UK plan—*'We don't have that yet'*—plus a framework whereby a programme on Namibia could be made. He found the African priority on Namibia at this point *'strange'*. The Insurance Fund could only be set up following basic minimum negotiating progress on Rhodesia.

FIRST ROUND: DAR ES SALAAM, 14–16 SEPTEMBER

Three days before Kissinger's arrival in the Tanzanian capital Nyerere had warned that the US initiative could be counter-productive,[70] since it was already being welcomed by Smith and interpreted by others as a gesture of support for white minority rule. The Americans' harping on their 'desire to stop communism' simply 'strengthens Smith in his determination to prevent majority rule'. Kissinger was met on his arrival by a student demonstration and was shocked to find that the Tanzanian Government had just released a statement urging the Americans to say that 'if peaceful transfer of power is impossible because of the intransigence of racists, then it will be on the side of those who fight for freedom'.[71] Kissinger complained to his aides that this kind of statement could sink his mission before he even got near Vorster or Smith. (On that very day Vorster and Smith were holding a crucial meeting in Pretoria where the SA Prime Minister was to 'soften up' the Rhodesian leader for the Kissinger 'bite' as he had promised in Zurich.) At the end of the first day of talks, Nyerere was not 'overhopeful' about the main issue on which he looked for success—Namibia. But he felt Kissinger had fully grasped the African position. Although Kissinger undertook to convey the FLPs' views to Pretoria on the Namibia issue, he was clearly focussing on Rhodesia. After the second day of talks Nyerere was still unhopeful about what could be achieved; but Kissinger less so.

NOTES FROM AN AUTHORITATIVE SOURCE

Nyerere argued with Kissinger that conditions were not ripe for hasty action in Rhodesia; but they were in Namibia where Vorster had the power to ordain change. So Kissinger should concentrate on Namibia when he got to Pretoria. Why couldn't Kissinger understand this? For his part, Kissinger explained that once Smith went, there should be a caretaker government with a black majority in Rhodesia, which Nyerere accepted. Then he proposed a Council of State, equivalent to the Governor, which would have a white majority. Nyerere said no; what would be acceptable was a 'Chissano Government'—something similar to the transitional government in Mozambique, where Frelimo named the members and the Portuguese appointed a High Commissioner. Kissinger seems to have accepted this formula, but said that Whitehall apparently preferred a Council to a single person, though he was trying to dissuade them. Such a government would in fact be of a caretaker nature, and would include whites. It would probably reflect across-the-board interests rather than be strictly of the Chissano type. Before leaving Dar, Kissinger told Nyerere: 'If you hear I have seen Smith it will be because Vorster has assured me that Smith accepts this thing' (i.e. the Anglo-American proposals).

ROUND TWO: LUSAKA, 16-17 SEPTEMBER

A fortnight before Kissinger's arrival in Zambia, Kenneth Kaunda had voiced his suspicions that the US might try and make a deal with Vorster, whereby majority rule in Rhodesia would be traded for acceptance of SA's own ideas about granting independence to Namibia. But he insisted there could be no trade-offs. 'We have made our stand very clear. Namibia must be free. Zimbabwe must be free on the basis of majority rule and apartheid must be cleared off the face of Africa.'[72]

'If you fail,' Kaunda told Kissinger with considerable emotion as they parted, 'we shall have reached the point of no return. God help you. We want to see peace, but peace with honour, peace with justice and freedom and independence. If we fail to get our demands peacefully, we must fight. We have no romantic views about an armed struggle.'

In Salisbury, the ruling Rhodesian Front Congress was giving Smith a noisy, unanimous and full mandate to participate in the US initiative to 'see what is on offer'. Smith had come back from Pretoria persuaded he must talk to Kissinger. 'Are you coming with me or not?' he demanded of his supporters. 'For God's sake be honest.'

NOTES FROM KISSINGER'S CONVERSATIONS EN ROUTE TO PRETORIA FROM LUSAKA (17 SEPTEMBER)

'If I didn't think it was possible that Smith would yield at some relatively early stage, I wouldn't be here. But I never said it was possible on this trip.'

ROUND THREE: PRETORIA, 17-18 SEPTEMBER

Fresh troubles and shootings were going on in Soweto as Kissinger flew in. Smith arrived on the same day—ostensibly to attend the rugby test match between SA and

New Zealand. In private conversation with the in-flight team of journalists, Kissinger said he would not see Smith to negotiate 'unless some clear result is in prospect: since that is not the case today (the 18th), there is nothing I can add.' However, he appeared to be more hopeful about some progress on Namibia by getting Vorster to agree to a round-table conference to which Swapo would be invited.

NOTES FROM KISSINGER'S CONVERSATIONS, PRETORIA (19 SEPTEMBER), EARLY MORNING
'Vorster has gone along on the whole with the basic approach we follow. The likelihood is that Smith is on the brink of making some decision. I expected that the SA riots would reduce Vorster's flexibility, but they haven't. My judgement is that we are on the road to significant progress. But I might have to take hell for a few weeks.' Kissinger added that Vorster had told him somewhat more than he had expected.

ROUND FOUR: PRETORIA, 19-20 SEPTEMBER
Kissinger decided over dinner with Vorster the previous night (Saturday, 18 September) that Smith was ready to make the necessary concessions; the only thing required were 'psychological reassurances' from Kissinger's own mouth about the bargaining that had already essentially been conducted through Vorster. Kissinger's press spokesman announced the meeting at one minute before midnight (Saturday) after flurried messages to the FLPs.

There had been nothing before this dramatic change of position to suggest that Smith was remotely contemplating giving up all he had stood for—and still believed in. He had led his rebellion to ensure the permanence of minority rule or, as he preferred to call it, 'the retention of government in civilized and responsible hands'. He had repeatedly reaffirmed this stand throughout 1976, beginning with his New Year statement in which he assured Rhodesians that he would not be party to any agreement 'that does not retain government in civilized and responsible hands'. In August when the Quenet Commission reported on ways of eliminating discrimination,[73] he scoffed at the idea of a common voters roll[74] and defended the Land Tenure Act, which divides land equally between the white minority and the overwhelming black majority. Whatever changes in discrimination were envisaged, he told the faithful, they should not be misinterpreted:[75] 'As far as we are concerned there can be no change and, indeed, there will be no fundamental change of the most fundamental of our principles—that of the retention of government in responsible hands.' In the middle of August, speaking on BBC radio, Smith again rejected majority rule: 'It would lead to a tragedy.'[76] This statement was made after Smith had been to see Vorster (2 August) following his return from Zurich. Finally, on the eve of Kissinger's shuttle to Africa, Smith said there was no such thing as 'the end of the road, defeat or surrender; Rhodesia had proved this over the past decade'.[77]

Now, unexpectedly, here was Vorster assuring Kissinger that if he met Smith he would be ready to 'offer the necessary concessions'. Their meeting was set for 10am on Sunday in the US Ambassador's residence.[78] Scheduled to last for an hour, it went on for four. According to senior American officials, Kissinger conducted the meeting by putting three principal questions to Smith: (1) How do you think Rhodesia can be rescued now that you know you have lost the last two friends on whose help white Rhodesians had been counting—South Africa and the United States? (2) If things are going so badly now, where do you think you will be next March, if the fighting is stepped up? (3) And if you think you will make it through next March, what about next year at this time? Kissinger then produced a summary of three sets of US intelligence reports about Rhodesia's military position. The Defence Intelligence Agency (DIA), the Intelligence and Research Bureau of the State Department (INR) and the Central Intelligence Agency (CIA). All three were in broad agreement; the only difference being their estimates of the time before Rhodesia's military and economic position finally collapsed. These US reports were confirmed by the military evaluation of the SA intelligence service, BOSS, which Vorster had previously given Smith. Faced with these bleak reports, Smith asked Kissinger what he expected of him. Kissinger then produced what he described as the 'British-American' plan, an elaboration of the terms laid down by Mr Callaghan in Parliament on 22 March. It was 2.00 pm when Smith said he wanted 'a few hours' to think over his reply.

The crunch meeting started at 5.40 pm. This time Vorster was present, and they met in the Prime Minister's official residence, 'Libertas', on the high hills over-looking Pretoria. Smith arrived looking tense and nervous. Kissinger was, by now, beginning to look tired. His voice was becoming hoarse, and there were uncharacteristic dark rings around his eyes. His fingernails, as always, were bitten to the quick. 'All I have to offer is my own head on a platter,' Smith began. Kissinger later spoke about the scene where the white Rhodesian surrender became final. He was full of admiration for the dignity shown by Smith and his men on what he described as 'the most painful day of their lives'.

The five points of agreement were accurately set out by Smith on 24 September,[79] though he deliberately interpreted them to give maximum reassurance to his white constituency about the way their position would be safeguarded during the transition to independence. The subsequent controversy about the proposals raised questions about whether secret assurances had been given by Kissinger as an inducement to Smith to accept majority rule. These issues are discussed below. The fact is that the two crucial proposals which subsequently wrecked the entire agreement were not discussed with the FLPs before they were conceded to Smith. The first was for a Council of State in the Interim Government to be composed of an equal number of whites and blacks with a white chairman. The second was for a Council of Ministers with a black majority, but with the Ministries of Law and Order (security) and Defence to be kept in white (Rhodesian) hands until independence. A two-thirds vote was required for decisions in both Councils. These two proposals were put forward by Smith as essential conditions for acceptance of the 'package' for majority rule. Kissinger was in a quandary: should he close the deal there and then, or should he postpone the decision until he could consult the FLPs? Callaghan and Wilson had warned him at the beginning of his shuttle not to make the mistake of letting Smith 'off the hook' if he ever had him on it; they reminded him that Smith had twice before gone into reverse after appearing to have agreed—in talks on the 'Tiger' and the 'Fearless'. 'Make him sign on the dotted line before he leaves the room.' was their advice. Thus, when Kissinger had Smith ready to concede the principle of majority rule, which all the African Presidents had said was unthinkable, he took a gamble. This was the only time during the entire diplomatic exercise that Kissinger abandoned the role of interlocutor. That he did so then was understandable. That he accepted those particular terms showed clearly that he had not understood the suspicions between blacks and whites in Rhodesia. Even if they were personally to accept the terms of the agreement, the FLPs would not be able to persuade the guerrilla leaders to lay down their arms in order to accept the authority of Smith's nominees for the Defence and Security posts. Perhaps Kissinger did understand this point, but thought Smith would not remain in politics, or could be removed. Vorster and the British, by contrast, took the view that only Smith could sell a rapid transfer to majority rule to white Rhodesians.

NOTES FROM KISSINGER'S CONVERSATIONS, PRETORIA, EN ROUTE TO LUSAKA (20 SEPTEMBER)

Responding to a question about Smith having talked of 'responsible' and not 'majority' rule: 'I want to make it quite clear that the US never had any concept in mind other than one-man-one-vote. The agreement is within the framework of proposals decided with the African Presidents and within the Anglo-American parameter. But it must be remembered that a lot of detail came up which had not been anticipated. (A reference to Smith's two crucial demands.) By the end of this week I will have a clear statement on the Rhodesian position that should go a very long way towards making negotiations possible. Assuming the black leaders stay within the framework of prior consultation, I believe a basis for consultation can be found.' Replying to a question whether the plan involved Smith stepping aside: 'I'm interested in principles. I don't care who carries them out. It would not be costless for Smith to double-cross me or "con" me in the presence of the SA Prime Minister who got us to talk in the first place.'

ROUND FIVE: LUSAKA, 20–21 SEPTEMBER

Kissinger was encouraged by the warmth of Kaunda's first reaction, but he reserved his final position until he first had a chance of studying the proposals in detail, and had consultations with the other FLPs as well as the black Rhodesian leaders. Kissinger had given him only one copy of the agreement, which had been immediately whisked away by the President's aides to make copies to be sent by a waiting courier to Machel in Maputo and to the Zimbabwean leaders.

NOTES ON CONVERSATIONS WITH KAUNDA/KISSINGER, LUSAKA EN ROUTE TO DAR ES SALAAM (21 SEPTEMBER)

'When Smith offered his head on a platter on Sunday he said that neither the white conservatives nor the blacks wanted him. What is happening now is a process that will continue with or without him. For what must have been the most painful day of their lives, the Rhodesians have behaved with great dignity . . . The key to breaking Smith was Vorster.'

ROUND SIX: DAR ES SALAAM, 21–22 SEPTEMBER

In contrast to the gloom of their last encounter, Nyerere was almost jubilant when he received Kissinger. He spoke of a 'breakthrough'; the Rhodesian question was 'drawing to an end'. But he was disappointed that there was no encouraging news about Namibia. Kissinger also had 15 minutes with Nkomo.

Meanwhile, in Salisbury, Smith was conferring with his Cabinet and caucus. He had received a message sent by Kissinger from Dar suggesting he was hopeful that the Africans would accept all the Pretoria proposals. It was this message, Smith later said, which convinced him to go ahead. The actual meaning of the message subsequently became a source of acute controversy (see Diplomatic Snafu below).

NOTES ON CONVERSATIONS WITH KAUNDA/KISSINGER, LUSAKA EN ROUTE TO DAR ES SALAAM (21 SEPTEMBER)

Nyerere's optimistic Press conference may make the decision for Smith more difficult in Salisbury. Nevertheless it was welcome as it would pre-empt Machel, Neto and the black Rhodesian groups.

ROUND SEVEN: ZAIRE, 22 SEPTEMBER

President Mobutu said Kissinger had 'convinced the Africans of the American solution instead of the African solution—armed struggle'. Kissinger left with the impression that he had 'the strong encouragement of Mobutu'.

THE DIPLOMATIC SNAFU: WHO WAS LYING?

A number of vital questions were in serious contention at the end of Kissinger's diplomatic shuffle. What secret understandings were reached with Vorster as a 'trade-off' for his support? What was the exact nature of the undertakings given to Kissinger by Smith in Pretoria? Was the agreement a 'package deal' which constituted a binding agreement on the US, UK and SA, even if it were later rejected by the Africans? Smith insists it was binding and that its terms were not negotiable. That undertaking, he says, was given to him in Pretoria, subject to the proviso that Kissinger would advise him whether it was acceptable to the FLPs before Smith committed himself in public. Kissinger had sent him a message from Dar es Salaam on 21 September which gave him the green light to go ahead and make his acceptance speech three days later. Three separate issues are involved in this argument: the negotiability of the terms; the binding nature of the agreement on the US *et al*; and whether the FLPs had reneged on Kissinger.

On the issue of whether the terms were negotiable (which became the major stumbling block at the Geneva Conference), Kissinger said right after the end of his shuttle, on 28 September, in an *NBC Today* interview: 'Obviously there will have to be negotiations for the transition . . . the composition of the Government, the allocation of Ministers, none of this has been settled yet. This requires negotiation.' On 8 October, speaking in 'The Week at the UN' programme, he said: 'I gave Ian Smith my best judgement of what would provide a framework and what might be acceptable'. Vorster agreed with Kissinger that the plan accepted by Smith was considered to be 'a basis for settlement discussions'.[80]

Were the terms binding? Did Kissinger give any secret undertakings in Pretoria about US support for Smith if the terms of the agreement were not observed by the Africans? In October 1976 a spokesman of the Smith regime claimed that 'it was made clear' to Smith during his talks with Kissinger that the US would show 'sympathy' towards Rhodesia if it accepted the terms for a settlement.[81] It added that US 'sympathy' was understood by the Smith regime to include support for the lifting of sanctions and 'logistical support' for its army; such support was primarily expected to take the form of helping it to obtain war supplies from other countries like France. This claim was firmly denied by Kissinger, speaking in President Carter's presence.[82] There was 'no possibility', he said, of the US selling arms to the white Rhodesians, even if talks broke down. Under pressure of questioning, Smith produced much vaguer answers about the supposed US undertaking.[83] 'It is a fact that in the talks I had with Dr Kissinger in Pretoria (19 September) at the commencement of this exercise, that he did give me an assurance that if we entered this agreement and it collapsed because of what the black Rhodesians had done, as opposed to myself and my government, that he was absolutely convinced that we would get a great deal more sympathy from the free world and also tangible assistance. And he believed it would lead to greater material support.' Pressed on whether the 'understanding' might include military supplies, the Rhodesian leader replied, 'Yes'. He added, however: 'I wouldn't say we have been given any hard and fast undertaking'. He added that no details were discussed.

Did Kissinger mislead Smith into believing that he had African support when he did not? According to Smith, the message he had received on 21 September from

Kissinger in Dar said that on the basis of his talks with Kaunda and Nyerere, he believed the provisions for having the Ministries of Law and Order and Defence in white hands 'can be added' to the other points agreed. In Smith's view, either the FLPs had reneged, or Kissinger had misled him. Bernard Gwertzman, the *New York Times* member of Kissinger's team of 'in-flight correspondents', reported that he had seen the actual text of the 21 September communication from Kissinger to Smith.[84] 'It was,' he wrote, 'an ambiguously worded instruction in a longer message and did not specifically say the black leaders had accepted the proposal; but it did leave that impression in both Pretoria and Salisbury.'

When Kissinger was asked in his *NBC Today* interview whether the African Presidents had rejected anything they told him they would approve, he replied: 'The African Presidents have not indicated a rejection of anything specific. The African Presidents have made a general statement that they will not accept the dictation of Smith with respect to all the details of the Transitional Government. On the other hand, what Smith has put forward was not his idea, but in itself reflected a compromise between many points of view.' Vorster thought Kissinger's reply 'a very remarkable statement'[85] in that it suggested the proposals that Mr Smith had announced were the result of discussions between the US, UK and black African Presidents *before* Kissinger had met Mr Smith.

On the same day that Kissinger gave his answer in the *NBC Today* interview, US officials acknowledged that 'details' of the settlement proposals were not accepted by the FLPs in advance of their submission to Smith. They admitted that the actual proposals were Kissinger's 'own refinements of terms for a peaceful settlement'.[86] Ted Rowlands, who succeeded David Ennals as the Minister of State for African Affairs, said that in his talks with Smith about settting up the Geneva Conference, he had talked specifically to him about the negotiability of the proposals; Smith had accepted that there would be a wide range of items on the agenda.[87] 'He even said he would have been surprised if I had suggested anything else. Therefore, it was clearly understood that the five-point plan was not, and could not, be the sole framework for a settlement.' The Rhodesian reply to Rowlands was that Smith had twice been promised by the British Government that it would persuade the Africans to accept the original proposals.[88] While it is true that the British thought the framework of the agreement offered a proper basis for a settlement, it never ruled out negotiations on the points of dispute.

What verdict can be made on the basis of this selection of the best evidence so far available? First, Smith admits that he was told in Pretoria that the settlement terms were subject to the Africans' approval. This, he says, was conveyed to him in Kissinger's September message from Dar. It was an ambiguous message undoubtedly drafted to encourage Smith to make his acceptance public; but it expressed only Kissinger's own *belief* (Smith confirmed this) that the terms would be accepted—not that they already had been. This seems very clear. Second, the claim that the terms were 'not negotiable'—the justification for Smith's stand at the Geneva Conference and afterwards—finds no supportive evidence from Kissinger, Vorster or the UK. Third, it is not in dispute that the FLPs had not seen the actual proposals before they were put to Smith; it is true that the initial reaction of Kaunda and Nyerere to Kissinger's news of Smith's acceptance of majority rule was enthusiastic; but both reserved their final decision until after the FLPs' meeting on 26 September. It was Kissinger's own 'best judgement' that they would accept—and this he transmitted to Smith. Whether he really was as hopeful as his message to Smith conveyed, or whether he was only gambling on a favourable outcome in order to push Smith towards publicly committing himself, will probably never be known. Finally, there is not the slightest evidence to suggest the Rhodesian claim of a secret deal between Smith and Kissinger over US arms or other support. Even the Rhodesians go no further than to suggest that the US would show 'sympathy' if they accepted the deal; their spokesman admits that it was the white Rhodesians themselves who interpreted this as meaning military support. And Smith confirms that he had not been given any 'hard and fast undertakings'.

The conclusion must be that Kissinger's subtle diplomacy led (or misled) Smith to believe much more than was actually conveyed in the crucial, but ambiguously-worded, signal sent on 21 September.

There is one last question: did Kissinger make any secret deals with Vorster to win over his support? Kissinger disavows any 'trade-off' of any kind. But there is more than just a suspicion that he assured the SA Prime Minister that the result (reward?) of his co-operating over Rhodesia and Namibia would be a diminishing of pressures on his regime by the US and other Western nations. If true, what might be the practical effects of 'diminished pressures'? Kissinger himself pulled no punches in continuing to attack apartheid and in urging the need for changes towards the goal of majority rule. A more likely 'trade-off' would be a refusal by Western governments to vote for tough resolutions in the Security Council. This, in fact, occurred when the US, UK and France together vetoed a proposal in the Security Council to make the arms embargo against SA compulsory. The private explanation for this action was that they did not wish to upset SA at a time when the negotiations over Namibia were still in the balance. Other possible US concessions to SA could be to restore the Republic to the list of approved countries for the guarantee arrangements provided by the US Export-Import Bank, and to give the green light to US bankers to raise loans for SA. Although Washington cannot dictate to bankers about foreign loans, the Administration's attitude to particular governments is nevertheless an important consideration in the calculations of bankers about the risks involved in making substantial foreign loans. After the Kissinger shuttle a Citibank consortium was engaged in raising a $100m loan for SA; but this proposal was apparently abandoned later. Instead, SA got a much bigger loan from a consortium of French bankers.

CLIMAX AND ANTI-CLIMAX: SMITH SAYS 'YES'; THE AFRICANS GIVE A QUALIFIED 'NO'

On 25 September, Smith broadcast to the nation his acceptance of 'majority rule within two years': the impossible had. become possible. He admitted frankly: 'I would be dishonest if I did not state quite clearly that the proposals that were put to us in Pretoria do not represent what in our view would be the best solution for Rhodesia's problems. Regrettably however, we were not able to make our views prevail, although we were able to achieve some modification in the proposals. The American and British Governments, together with the major Western Powers have made up their minds as to the kind of solution they are determined to bring about. The alternative to acceptance of the proposals was explained to us in the clearest of terms which left no room for misunderstanding . . . What I have said this evening will be the cause of deep concern to you all and understandably so, but we live in a world of rapid change, and if we are to survive in such a world we must be prepared to adapt ourselves to change'.[89] Mr Smith closed by quoting Churchill: 'This is not the end. It is not even the beginning of the end, but it is perhaps the end of the beginning.'

On 26 September the five FLPs met in Lusaka. They 'hailed and congratulated' the people and fighters of Zimbabwe who had 'forced the rebel regime and the enemy in general to recognize and accept the inevitability of majority rule . . .' But they declared that to accept the proposals as set forth by Smith would be 'tantamount to legalizing the colonialist and racist structures of power'. Instead, they asked the British Government to convene a conference 'with the authentic and legitimate representatives of the people' to discuss the structure and functions of the transitional government'.[90] Rightly, Kissinger saw this statement as rather more than half a victory. The ball was now back in the British court. The Salisbury regime complained that it had been misinformed or misled by the US. Reactions in most other African capitals were strongly supportive of the FLPs. The Nigerian Government said the settlement proposals had 'failed to satisfy the most basic democratic principles'. The Sudan Government expressed 'complete satisfaction with the intensified and commendable efforts of the five FLPs. The Ghana Supreme Military Council said it opposed any relaxation of the pressures on the Smith regime. Only Angola's President Neto took a position out of line with the other FLPs. On the day after the Lusaka summit he said: 'The initiative for liberation of peoples can never emanate from the US which is an imperialist country . . . it was necessary to reject all North American efforts aimed at taking the initiative on the liberation of Namibia and Zimbabwe. Such initiatives belonged to those peoples or to the African countries . . .'[91] A similar view was expressed by Radio Maputo: 'This so-called Anglo-American plan is intended to sabotage our (Zimbabwe people's) revolution . . . the Zimbabwean people under the vanguard leadership of the revolutionary organization, Zipa, must reject out of hand this present manoeuvre by the Anglo-Americans'.[92] Zipa had already done so five days earlier at a Press Conference in Maputo. 'We are determined,' they said, 'to fight the Kissinger proposals to the bitter end'.[93] Nkomo found 'serious flaws' in the proposals. So did all the other Zimbabwe Nationalists. But none went so far as Amin in suggesting: 'I would have been happier if the visit had been undertaken by countries like the Soviet Union, China, Yugoslavia and Cuba or even some few Western countries who assisted Liberation Movements'.[94]

THE ROAD TO GENEVA: BRITAIN'S RELUCTANT ROLE IN 1976

The British Government—wearied by some 11 years of futile attempts to rid itself as painlessly as possible of the Rhodesian albatross from its post-imperial neck, and overwhelmed at home by economic crisis and the relentless Ulster ulcer—had been delighted by the opportunity of handing over the burden to the Americans. The one thing it did not want to emerge from Kissinger's initiative was a resumption of an active role for Britain in Rhodesia. David Spanier, the Diplomatic Correspondent of *The Times*, closely reflected the official British mind when he wrote on 23 September: 'The Government has decided, whatever the outcome of Dr Kissinger's mission that there is no question of a British Governor-General or British judges or British civil servants being sent out to Rhodesia to assist in the transitional arrangements, still less British troops'. It is essential to understand this attitude in trying to follow the shifts of British policy up to and through the Geneva talks. Britain wanted to do no more than it decently had to do, but in the end found itself forced to take on much more than it had contemplated before Kissinger's initiative. As late as 2 January 1977, the British Premier had this to say in a BBC radio interview: 'I'm not very anxious to go in at all. Rhodesia has not been a British colony for years and years and years. But if we have got a role to play that does not involve us in stretching ourselves beyond our capacity and our strength, then we have got a responsibility to do it . . . We've got to husband our resources. We've got plenty to do here to get our situation right.'

Convening a constitutional conference for Rhodesia fell easily within the acceptable limits of British responsibility. When, on 26 September, the FLPs pressed for a conference to be called, the late Foreign Secretary, Anthony Crosland, responded on the very next day. And just one day later, Ted Rowlands went to Africa to negotiate the details, accompanied by William Schaufele, the US Assistant Secretary for African Affairs who had played a key role in Kissinger's shuttle. Smith himself took the initiative in proposing that Rowlands should visit Salisbury. Nkomo, Muzorewa, Sithole and Chikerema all welcomed a constitutional conference under British chairmanship. Nobody objected to Smith being invited.

Rowlands had to achieve three results to rescue Kissinger's initiative: get quick agreement to the conference being convened in order to keep up the momentum; ensure that it would be fully representative; and persuade Smith that the whole 'package' was still negotiable. Although Smith accused the British of 'changing the terms', he nevertheless agreed to come. The FLPs skilfully brought the rival black nationalists across the hurdles; even those committed to the sole tactic of 'armed struggle' agreed not only to come, but to sit down with the 'enemy' Smith—no mean feat. At the beginning of October the British Foreign Secretary spoke of the 'awesomely high stakes' if the initiative failed.[95] 'The war,' he said, 'would escalate; Rhodesia would be plunged into economic chaos and so would the surrounding African States; the South Africans would intervene on one side and, possibly, the Cubans on the other'. By 12 October, he was able to declare that the road to Geneva was open, but his subsequent announcement that the conference would be chaired, not by himself, but by the UK Ambassador to the UN, Ivor Richard, almost scuppered the talks: the Africans questioned whether Britain was committed at a high enough level to the success of the conference.

THE GENEVA CONFERENCE—IN WHICH CHAIRMAN MAO IS PROVED RIGHT
'You cannot win at the conference table what you have not won on the battlefield'—Chairman Mao-tse Tung

The Geneva Conference never stood much of a chance of producing a final constitutional settlement, but it was nevertheless essential for three reasons: to keep a diplomatic initiative alive; to prove genuine African interest in a peaceful alternative to guerrilla warfare; and to establish the minimum conditions for an agreement acceptable to black and white Rhodesians for a transitional government leading to independence. The talks contributed to all three objectives. At the end of the conference, a new diplomatic initiative was still possible; the FLPs and the nationalists had proved their interest in negotiating for a transitional Government. It also revealed that the gulf which separated the two sides could not be bridged by the Kissinger proposals.

Geneva turned out to be another arena for the Rhodesian struggle in which the protagonists sought to demonstrate their respective strengths. Both sides sought to enhance their bargaining positions at the conference table by escalating the fighting on the actual battleground. This showed that the Rhodesian forces were not yet defeated, nor even as weak as Smith's political surrender to Kissinger in Pretoria might have suggested; the Zimbabweans could not force Smith's capitulation when they had not yet finally won victory on the battlefield.

When the conference finally got under way on 28 October, the guerrillas took the initiative in the field by launching heavy new attacks, but by the end of the conference the military initiative had passed back into Smith's hands. October turned out to be the bloodiest month in the fighting so far with the deaths of 15 Rhodesian soldiers and 144 guerrillas, and 84 civilian fatalities. In November, he sharply escalated the fighting by penetrating deep into Mozambique to strike at the guerrilla camps—a tactic repeated twice in quick succession. These attacks achieved three results: they inflicted heavy losses on the guerrillas, but even worse on Zimbabwe and Mozambique civilians;[96] they exposed the weakness in Mozambique's defences which forced Machel to re-examine the need for external military support; and they boosted the flagging morale of white Rhodesians. Suddenly, defeat no longer seemed inevitable. The Rhodesian tactic of hitting the guerrillas at the rear was militarily sound, but the political risks were high. These were that Mozambique would be compelled to call in foreign military aid to speed up the training of its still scratch army, and to strengthen its border defences. The question was whether Machel would seek African military support (he already had help from the Tanzanian army), or turn to the Russians, Cubans or Chinese—thus introducing the very element of international involvement which the Geneva Conference was designed to avoid. It soon became clear that Smith's military and political tactics were closely linked.

SMITH'S NEW STRATEGY

From the day the conference began Smith took the stand that there was nothing to negotiate other than the implementation of his agreement with Kissinger. If the 'terrorists' and 'militant Marxists' were willing to talk on those terms, he was available; otherwise he was 'not interested in their antics'. Britain and the US, he insisted, had made a solemn agreement with him. As 'a man of his word' *he* was prepared to stand by that agreement; but were the others? When both the British and the Americans insisted that the terms of the agreement had to be negotiated, he announced a new policy. He would abandon the Geneva conference, and implement the agreement unilaterally. Once having fulfilled his side of the bargain to bring about majority rule—in co-operation with 'moderate Africans'—he would expect SA, the US and, less hopefully, the British, to honour their side.

There was another and more dangerous element in Smith's tactics which emerged from the briefings provided by himself and his Foreign Minister, Piet van der Byl. In their view, once Communist forces appeared in any numbers in Mozambique, SA would be compelled to enter the fighting on his side—and when that happened, the US would follow. So the success of Smith's strategy depended on Mozambique and Zipa bringing in the Communists—and the best chance of producing that result was for the Rhodesian troops to continue striking deep into Mozambique. In the Walter Mitty world inhabited by white Rhodesians this kind of thinking sounded less strange than elsewhere. There is undoubtedly some reality in the assumption that SA might blunder back into Rhodesia if Communist forces appeared in Mozambique; but who could believe that the US—especially a Carter Administration—would become involved in a second Vietnam? Yet it was Smith who tirelessly accused Mugabe and the others at Geneva of 'living in Cloud Cuckooland'.

WHO SPEAKS FOR THE AFRICANS?

The Africans' position at Geneva was much more complex than Smith's straightforward and monolithic role. First, there were the three rival groups—the Patriotic Front, the Bishop's ANC and Sithole's Zanu rump—each pursuing its own tactics about how to achieve their agreed objective. Although outwardly united, Nkomo and Mugabe were also engaged in a power struggle over who would finally lead the country. Although the spokesman for Zanu/Zipa, Mugabe was under strong constraints not to go further towards negotiation than his constituency—the military cadres—were prepared for. He still needed to consolidate his political leadership within Zipa.

At the start of the conference Zipa contented itself with an observer's role. A small delegation included the former Zanu commander, Josiah Tongogara, who had been specially released by a Zambian court in the middle of his trial for Chitepo's murder.[97] Two other Zanu leaders released at the same time accompanied him. Zipa's new military commander, Rex Nhongo, also put in a brief appearance. Although they shared Mugabe's suite of rooms in the Intercontinental Hotel, they were not part of the Patriotic Front's delegation. It was not until the beginning of December that Rex Nhongo brought over a Zipa delegation to 'ensure and protect the independence of the people of Zimbabwe from being sabotaged and hijacked by imperialists, their racist allies and the apologists of imperialism, and to ensure the people's independence against the personal political ambitions of the opportunists and apologists of monopoly capitalism.' Zipa's decision to send a delegation was prompted by two reasons: differences had arisen between Mugabe and Nkomo over the question of whether elections should be held before independence (see below); and there were growing suspicions of a possible 'deal' between Muzorewa, Smith and the British.

Except for Angola, all the ringmasters were also present on the sidelines to keep a watchful eye and, when necessary, to nudge the Zimbabweans into making the tactical concessions necessary to prevent the talks from collapsing. Also on the sidelines were the Americans, playing a similar role vis-à-vis the British.

The Salisbury delegation were reluctant participants playing a spoiling role. Smith himself put in only two brief appearances at the beginning and at the end. His men sniped at the British chairman and at the Zimbabweans. 'Marxist terrorist murderers' was the phrase used by van der Byl in referring to Mugabe and his colleagues. Their strategy was to wait for the black delegations to break ranks and fight each other, which they believed would inevitably happen.[98]

The only real negotiations that took place were between the British and the Zimbabweans. It took them a full month to overcome the first hurdle—a decision on the date for independence. The Patriotic Front had insisted it should be fixed as an *a priori* condition for discussing the form of the Interim Government. In the end, by a complicated formula,[99] agreement was reached fixing the date for independence on 1 March 1978. This agreement came only as a result of quiet but firm pressures by the FLPs on both the Patriotic Front and the British, and after a joint public demand by Tanzania and Nigeria for the date to be fixed.[100]

PROPOSALS FOR A TRANSITIONAL GOVERNMENT

During the long deadlock, which was broken only on 29 November, all the delegations (including Smith's) had circulated their proposals for the composition of the Interim Government. The Patriotic Front proposed that there should be no Council of State (as envisaged in the Kissinger proposals), but only a single Council of Ministers with full legislative and executive powers, the majority of whom (including the PM) would be drawn from the Liberation Movement. They would control, directly or indirectly, all the Ministries concerned with completing the pre-independence process, including Law and Order and Defence. The Bishop's ANC delegation wanted the Interim Government to be formed after the popular election of a PM, who would form a Cabinet composed of the different groups contesting the election. A British Governor would be installed for the transition, and would preside over a National Security Council responsible for producing a national army.

Sithole proposed a single-tier government with a Presidium and Council of Ministers. The Presidium would be composed of all the delegates at Geneva; and each would appoint four members of the Council of Ministers. A separate Defence Council would be made up of leading representatives from the conference. The Salisbury regime presented a detailed 8-stage plan to implement the Kissinger proposals within 23–25 months.[101] The British introduced an 11-stage plan to implement whatever agreement was reached at Geneva.[102] The British proposals were concerned only with the mechanism for the transition to independence; they included no independent views about the shape of the Interim Government itself.

A crucial difference of opinion arose between Mugabe and Nkomo at the end of November over whether general elections should form part of the process of independence; the latter insisted on elections, while the former took the view that power at independence must pass automatically to the Liberation Movement (as had occurred in Mozambique with Frelimo). Mugabe felt he could not accept Nkomo's proposal without returning for consultations with the Zipa leadership in Maputo. It was after his visit that Zipa sent its independent delegation to Geneva to stop the 'imperialist intrigues'. No finality was reached on this issue by the end of the conference, although President Machel later supported Nkomo's stand on elections (see below).

Muzorewa seized on the issue of popular elections in Zimbabwe to decide who should lead the country during the transition period, and this sharply divided the Zimbabwean ranks. It also brought Smith down in favour of an elected black leader, because he expected the Patriotic Front, and especially Mugabe, to come off worst in an election.

WHAT ROLE FOR BRITAIN?

'Whatever is going to happen will be decided by forces over which we have no control and over which we can make no projections'—Enoch Powell, 21 October 1976

The FLPs, meeting in Lusaka on 17 October, called on Britain to assume its obligations as the colonial power in Rhodesia, not only at the Geneva conference but also during the transition period. Nyerere explained that they wanted a British Governor-General, or similar figure, to be the ultimate authority during that period.[103] This African call for Britain to return—for a time—as the colonial ruler gladdened few British hearts. Only the Conservatives supported the idea of a resumption of British imperial responsibility—a demand made on a number of occasions by the Shadow Foreign Secretary, Reginald Maudling.[104] But in his view, the purpose of such a British role would be to assist Smith to implement the Kissinger proposals and to resist the guerrillas. The Tories' lunatic fringe, led by MPs like Ronald Bell and Julian Amery, went much further in calling for a strong British military commitment openly to support the Smith regime; the former even spoke of a British military base in Rhodesia. But such ideas found little response in the British mood of the 1970s. The experience of Ulster had bred a strong resistance to any new British commitment which would put it in a position of having to exercise 'responsibility without power'—and of being shot at by both sides.

Such anxieties were amply confirmed by the British chairman's experience at Geneva. White Rhodesian attitudes were predictably caustic. Nkomo, Mugabe and Muzorewa all, in turn, accused Richard of favouring the other side, and of 'imperialist trickery'. At the end of November, the Patriotic Front issued a formal statement alleging that Anglo-American 'imperialists' wanted to 'replace the Smith regime by a black regime which will be less exposed to attack, but will serve their interests even more efficiently'. The thought behind this suspicion was that Muzorewa was being favoured to produce a moderate government at independence. Just a month later the Bishop made an attack in almost identical terms—though naturally his suspicion was that Britain and the FLPs were working for a Patriotic Front victory. Yet despite these attacks, all the black nationalists insisted, along with the FLPs, that the only way to break the deadlock over who would exercise effective authority during the transition period was through a British presence. Because the Africans totally rejected the idea of defence and security being in white Rhodesian hands, and because the Smith regime would not entrust them to black hands, the obvious compromise was to restore to Britain the authority which it had legally exercised in the colony until UDI. This view was vigorously resisted only by the Rhodesia Front. But other white Rhodesian leaders, like Sir Roy Welensky, felt that a British role was essential. So did Garfield Todd, a former Rhodesian Prime Minister. (Along with Justice Leo Baron and Dr Ruth Palley, he was acting as an advisor to Nkomo's delegation in Geneva. Dr Ahrn Palley, another white Rhodesian exile, was an advisor to Muzorewa's delegation.)

As Geneva moved heavily from one deadlocked position to the next—while Rhodesia moved towards more concentrated fighting—the initial British resistance to any idea of becoming involved during the transition period began to weaken. The US threw its weight behind the FLPs' demands for Britain to accept an active role in the Interim Government. A lively debate in the British Press also began to reflect growing support for Britain to reassume its legal responsibility for the rebel colony. By the end of November, Ivor Richard had decided that progress was impossible without a new British commitment. 'Re-enter the Governor of Rhodesia?' *The Times* asked in a forward-looking editorial on 23 November. Five days later the Conservatives' new Shadow Foreign Secretary, John Davies, gave his party's conditional support to the idea of a British Governor for Rhodesia. On the same day, the influential US Senator, Dick Clark, chairman of the Senate's Africa sub-committee, declared that the UK had to assume 'at least some of the residual powers that they had before'. On 2 December, Crosland informed Parliament of HMG's readiness to play 'a direct role in the transitional government'; but he added that 'the nature of this British presence would, of course, depend on the structure agreed for the Interim Government.' So, less than two months after the frosty reception given to Nyerere's call on behalf of the FLPs, Westminster had reversed itself —pushed by its friends in Africa and by the US, and encouraged by the Zimbabwe nationalists—but, above all, frightened by the consequences of what could happen if Geneva collapsed for want of a new British initiative.

THE END OF GENEVA
By the beginning of December it was clear that nothing more could be expected from the Geneva talks at that stage. Neither Smith nor his opponents were willing to yield an inch on any of the vital points which divided them: the rival proposals for an Interim Government were irreconcilable so long as Smith continued to stand on his 'package'; the anticipated rift in the black lute had developed between Muzorewa's camp and the Patriotic Front, though the Mugabe-Nkomo alliance had survived intact despite their differences; the British had accepted the new role thrust on them; and the war in Rhodesia was becoming more worrying by the day. Only renewed pressures on the Smith regime—through a combination of diplomacy, the armed struggle and economic blockade—could improve the chances for a negotiated settlement.

Kissinger, on his round of farewells, flew to London on 10 December and said the initiative must remain with Britain. Speaking at a meeting of Nato Defence Ministers on 10 December, Crosland spoke of his preference for a 'moderate' nationalist government to emerge in Zimbabwe rather than 'a Marxist military dictatorship'. The Patriotic Front leaders took this to confirm their suspicions about secret British support for Muzorewa. On the last day of the conference, Mugabe and Nkomo in a joint statement accused Britain and the US of trying to create a puppet regime in Rhodesia. On this sour note Ivor Richard formally adjourned the conference on 14 December until 17 January 1977. On the same day Crosland announced that Richard would leave for Africa immediately after Christmas on a new mission to try and retrieve the Kissinger initiative.

A NEW BRITISH INITIATIVE: THIS TIME SMITH SAYS 'NO', THE AFRICANS SAY 'PERHAPS'

Ivor Richard unfolded the Anglo-American Mark Two proposals for a settlement on 23 December 1976 in Washington, having previously received US backing as well as Kissinger's personal endorsement. The new plan offered Zimbabweans a choice of four options: (1) Direct control by a British representative of the key posts of Defence and Law and Order in the transition Government. (2) A National Security Council with an equal number of white and black representatives and 'a neutral chairman'. (3) One of the key posts to go to a black representative and the other to a white representative. (4) One minister to control both portfolios; he would be white, but not a member of the Rhodesian Front. Whichever option was chosen, Whitehall would provide a British Commissioner as the interim Head of State. There would be no British troops under any circumstances, but there would be an administrative back-up for the Commissioner. A Commonwealth force, too, was ruled out. The central issue of how finally to integrate the guerrilla forces and the Rhodesian army could, in Richard's view, be done only by agreement and consensus: with the political leaders on both sides agreeing that the war should stop, the two forces would at least come together and eventually integrate after independence.

In the first round of his visits to the capitals of the FLPs (but not to Luanda) the new proposals got a fair wind, but the Zimbabwean leaders were harder to tie down. Eventually, on 17 January 1977, the Patriotic Front said that they could make a firm decision only after the final British proposal was put on paper 'clearly and precisely'. In other words, they wanted the British to indicate which of the four options was to be implemented. This at least indicated a readiness to negotiate further. Subsequently Britain did provide more detailed proposals (see below).

When Richard had the first of his two meetings with Vorster he found him unwilling to commit himself to the merits of the plan until he had received categorical assurances from the FLPs that the armed struggle would stop once an agreement was reached. Richard's second round of visits produced firm commitments from Nyerere, Kaunda, Machel and Khama. When he left Dar es Salaam he said he had 'run out of adjectives' to describe how good his meeting had been with Nyerere. But it was in Maputo that Richard scored his biggest triumph, when Machel declared: 'The principle of independence is no longer questioned. Now it is a question of finding the modalities to implement this principle. War is fed by blood and it destroys lives. We therefore say welcome to the chairman of the conference, welcome to Great Britain. We hope you will find all the necessary co-operation'.

The story was different in Salisbury. Even in advance of Richard's arrival, the Foreign Affairs Ministry had dealt a rebuff to the British proposals in a 10-page background briefing which rejected any British role in the transition period and which accused the British of being 'patently out of touch with the realities of the situation' in Rhodesia. The first encounter with Smith on 2 January 1977 produced what Richard later described as 'a good verbal punch-up'. A Rhodesian paper described Smith as having adopted a 'snarling' attitude which had led Richard to lose his temper.

In the middle of his second round of talks on 9 January, the FLPs at a meeting in Lusaka announced their exclusive recognition for the Patriotic Front. This decision was intended to strengthen the unity of the Zimbabwean fighting front, but it had two serious results. The first was that it virtually ensured Smith's rejection of the British proposals since the implications of the FLPs' recognition meant that effective power would pass into the hands of Mugabe and Nkomo, with the former possibly in the stronger position. The second result was that, so far from unifying the Zimbabweans, it widened the rift between Muzorewa's supporters and the Patriotic Front. The decision forced Muzorewa to pursue his own independent initiative inside Rhodesia—just as Nkomo had done a year earlier.

Meanwhile, Richard was able to return to SA carrying with him the FLPs' unequivocal assurances that the fighting would stop once a Transition Government was installed. This time he got Vorster's support for the proposals, and found him as determined as ever to avert a full-scale war in Rhodesia. Back in Salisbury, he had a friendlier meeting with Smith. But on 24 January, Smith broadcast his total rejection of the British proposals. 'My military chiefs,' he said, 'were horrified'. His Foreign Minister described the British terms as being 'worse than those for the Nazis. They were so intolerable that you would fight even if there was no hope.' Smith still insisted that a settlement would be reached only by implementing his 'agreement' with Kissinger. The British Foreign Secretary told Parliament that Smith's rejection of the proposals—the only one to do so—represented 'a serious setback to all their hopes for peace'. The Conservative spokesmen, John Davies and Reginald Maudling, put the blame for the setback, not on Smith, but on the British Government.

The militants on both sides were, once again, firmly in control of their forces. Cries of 'good old Smithy' were once again popular in Salisbury.[105] 'It would be better to die to the last man and the last cartridge than to die in front of one of Mugabe's People's Courts,' was the view of a typical Smith hardliner—his Foreign Minister, P. J. van der Byl.[106] But there were also some saner voices in Rhodesia who thought 'Smith must be crazy'.[107] Sir Roy Welensky insisted that there was no alternative to accepting a British presence. The three white Opposition groups—Rhodesia Party, Centre Party and the National Pledge Association—joined forces to form a pressure group to back a negotiated settlement. And a handful of white Rhodesians carried placards in a demonstration calling for a peaceful end to the fighting.

BRITAIN'S PROPOSALS FOR A TRANSITION GOVERNMENT

Ivor Richard handed over the following Note to the Geneva delegations 'for further discussion and negotiation':

'In formulating these ideas the British Government have attempted to meet the general concern that the process of transition to independence should be rapid, guaranteed, and orderly. It is the particular concern of the nationalists that the minority should not be able to exercise such a control over the transitional government as to allow it either to delay independence or so to influence the drawing-up of the independence constitution as to prevent it from giving full effect to genuine majority rule. It is the particular concern of the minority that there will be a genuine transitional period, during which the security situation will be properly controlled, and that there will be a place for them in an independent Zimbabwe.

'In pursuance of these interests, the two sides in the negotiations have hitherto adopted incompatible positions concerning the power-structure during the transitional period: the nationalists have pressed for an immediate transfer of full power to themselves; the minority have insisted on a structure for the transitional government which would have the effect of leaving control over the vital areas in their own hands. In the view of the British Government both of these positions are unrealistic. A negotiated settlement is possible only if both sides agree to a structure for the transitional government which strikes a reasonable balance between them and which gives adequate protection to the legitimate interests of both. This would have to provide for a visible and effective African majority in the government but also for a participation by representatives of the European minority sufficient to ensure that their interests were taken into account. While power in sensitive areas, such as internal security and the drawing-up of the independence constitution, could not be left in minority hands, it should not pass, during the transitional period, wholly into the hands of the nationalists.

'The suggestions in this paper are designed to provide such a structure. They proceed on the basis that where solutions can be found using purely Rhodesian elements, that should be done. But where that is not possible, it is suggested that a British presence could usefully be introduced to assure each side that neither can prevent the achievement of the legitimate aims of the other. There would have to be a number of pre-conditions for the introduction of any British presence into the constitutional arrangements for Rhodesia during the transitional period. Among the most important of these would be that it was clearly accepted by all parties concerned that guerrilla activity would cease as soon as agreement had been reached on the setting up of the transitional government; and British readiness to continue to play a part in the agreed transitional arrangements would be conditional upon all other parties abiding by that agreement.

'In the light of the above considerations, the British Government suggests that the parties should now discuss a structure for the transitional government of Rhodesia on the following lines: the transitional government would be headed by an interim commissioner who would be appointed by the British Government, after due consultations. There would also be a deputy interim commissioner, appointed in the same way, who would act as interim commissioner whenever the former was unable to do so. In addition to the interim commissioner, the transitional government would have three principal organs:

(a) A Council of Ministers.
(b) An Advisory Council of senior Ministers.
(c) A National Security Council.

'The Council of Ministers would contain equal numbers of members from each of the political groups represented by the delegations to the Geneva conference and a further similar number of members appointed by the Interim Commissioner from among members of the European minority. It would thus have a substantial African majority. The leaders of the delegations to the Geneva conference would be members of the council of ministers and would together form an Inner Cabinet (perhaps called the Advisory Council) which would act in a general advisory capacity to the Interim Commissioner and would also have other specified functions.

'The Council of Ministers would have full executive and legislative competence for the Government of Rhodesia, subject only to the Interim Commissioner's reserve powers.

'Except where his reserve powers were involved, the Interim Commissioner would be required to act in accordance with the advice of his Ministers in exercising all his executive functions and in assenting to legislation. If there were agreement on the choice of one of the African members of the Council of Ministers as a First Minister, the meetings of the Council of Ministers would be presided over by the

First Minister who would, as such, also have other specified functions. If not, other arrangements would have to be made: e.g. the chairmanship of meetings of the Council of Ministers might rotate among the members of the Advisory Council. In any event, the person presiding over the Council of Ministers would not have a casting vote.

'The Interim Commissioner would not be a member of the Council of Ministers and would ordinarily not attend its meetings. However, he would be empowered to do so when he considered that matters might be discussed which could affect his residual responsibilities (see paragraph below).

'The Interim Commissioner would have residual responsibility for certain subjects (primarily external affairs, defence, internal security and the implementation of the programme for independence). His powers in the Council of Ministers in relation to these subjects would enable him to ensure, on the one hand, that the minority in the Council of Ministers could not impede the transition to majority rule and independence and, on the other hand, that the Transitional Government did not act in a way which would imperil the orderly nature of that transition or which was incompatible with the exercise of the United Kingdom's constitutional responsibilities.

'The question of voting procedures in the Council of Ministers could be regulated in a number of different ways. In choosing the appropriate voting system, the aim should be to ensure that the will of the substantial majority of the members of the Council of Ministers prevailed in matters of day-to-day government and in maintaining the momentum of the transition to majority rule and independence; but also to ensure that the representatives of the minority community, while not being able to impede that transition, were given an effective voice in all decisions of special concern to their community. Where the Interim Commissioner's residual responsibilities were involved, a special majority would be required and the Interim Commissioner would himself be given a vote which, in certain situations, could operate as a casting vote. Apart perhaps from defence and internal security (see paragraph below) and possibly also external affairs, all departments of government would be in the charge of a Minister. The Council of Ministers would have collective responsibility for governing Rhodesia.

'Defence and internal security would be the responsibility of the National Security Council, though this would not necessarily preclude the allocation of these portfolios to individual ministers if agreement on that matter could be reached. The Council would consist of the Interim Commissioner (and perhaps also the deputy Interim Commissioner); the leading members of the Council of Ministers; and the two chiefs of staff of the armed forces and the Commissioner of Police. These three officers would themselves be appointed and removable by the Interim Commissioner. The Interim Commissioner would preside over meetings of the National Security Council and would be in a position to exercise a casting vote.

'The day-to-day organization and operational control of the armed forces and the police would be the responsibility of the respective chiefs of staff and the Commissioner of Police. But these would be responsible (either directly or, if there were ministers for defence and internal security, through those Ministers) to the National Security Council which would give them general directives of policy with regard to the maintenance of public security and generally with regard to the organization and employment of the forces under their command.

'The National Security Council, with the concurrence of the Interim Commissioner, would have the power to appoint and remove the holders of certain senior offices in the armed forces and the police. The National Security Council would also be responsible for supervising the reorganization of the defence and internal security forces.

'The Council of Ministers would be responsible for the implementation of the programme for independence and in particular for the working out of the independence constitution. For this purpose, it would appoint a constitutional committee which would include representatives of the various political parties and also constitutional and other experts (perhaps from outside Rhodesia). The constitutional committee would formulate recommendations to the Council of Ministers. The Interim Commissioner would himself preside over the constitutional committee (as well, of course as taking part in the consideration of its recommendation in the Council of Ministers).

THE MERCENARY FACTOR IN THE RHODESIAN CONFLICT

'Would you like to work in fun? Then come and join the Rhodesian Army'—Advertisement for foreign volunteers

The SA Prime Minister has refused to commit himself in advance about the role of the Republic's army if the war is not checked in Rhodesia. He insists that the final decision, if one ever has to be taken, will be made by Parliament. But Africa is already concerned with a different aspect of this question: even if SA or the Western nations do not intervene openly, what clandestine role might they play? Their suspicions are reinforced by the influx of 'volunteers' or 'mercenaries'. No matter which description one cares to apply to the foreign recruits in the Rhodesian army, this element is certain to become a crucial factor in relations between Africa and the West. The emotional response from both sides over this question was shown at the time of the trial of 'mercenaries' in Angola in 1976,[108] and in Rhodesia feelings will be much stronger for three reasons. First, SA could exercise the softer 'option' of allowing its soldiers to enlist in Smith's army, rather than fight in their own uniforms. Second, there is already evidence of a considerable 'volunteer force' of whites going to the defence of white Rhodesia. (The current rate of pay for volunteers is roughly $4,000 a year for privates, $6,400 for sergeants and $7,600 for junior officers.) Third, since the actual number of regular soldiers in the Rhodesian army is very small, it will not take a large influx of volunteers to give it the character of a foreign white army.

Just how many foreigners already form part of the Rhodesian army's 6,000 regulars? According to Hugh Lynn, a British deserter from the Rhodesian army, there were 2,000 Britons in 1976, many of them former paratroopers, and over 100 Americans, mostly Vietnam veterans. In a Botswana radio interview, two other army deserters corroborated the estimate that about a third of the regular forces are already made up of foreign volunteers. Robin Wright, reporting from Salisbury, put the number of foreign recruits at 1,000, with volunteers coming from Germany, Canada, Greece, Holland, Australia, Portugal, France, New Zealand, Britain, Sweden—and even one from Sri Lanka.[109] She put the American contingent at 400. A South African reporter, Paul Smurthwaite, also put the American contingent at 400. He supported the overall figure of 1,000.[110] There are 20 Australians, mostly Vietnam veterans fighting in Rhodesia; an Australian TV unit which filmed them was deported in early 1977.

There are no reliable estimates of the number of recruits from SA, only hints about their existence. A 25-year old soldier sentenced to death in December 1976 for the murder of a black taxi-driver was said in court to have been South African. The Lisbon paper *Diario de Lisboa* (December 1976) reported that recruits for the Rhodesian forces were being trained at Iscar, near Valladolid in Spain. This is the camp of the so-called Guerrillas of Christ the King and the Adolf Hitler Commando who are involved in Portugal's own clandestine counter-revolutionary movement. According to the Lisbon report, some units were also being trained there to go to Rhodesia for operations against Mozambique. A similar military element is being provided by the Mozambique United Front according to the Voice of Free Africa, an anti-Frelimo radio station which broadcasts from Rhodesia. This force is believed to include both white and black opponents of Machel's regime.[111]

The Tanzanian Government paper, *Daily News*, reported in December 1976 that 1,500 mercenaries had been recruited abroad. It doubted whether such recruitment could have been undertaken without prior knowledge of the governments concerned. For their own reasons, the Russians have made a regular feature in Radio Moscow of reports to Africa about 'Western mercenaries' in Rhodesia.

Major Nick Lamprecht, Rhodesia's chief army recruiting officer, has denied that the foreigners are 'mercenaries'.[112] He explains their motive as 'enthusiasm about fighting communism—they don't want to see a repeat of what happened in Vietnam'.

Major Lamprecht's 22-year old son, Vincent, took a totally opposite view from his father's. After completing his own national service he emigrated to South Africa where he said: 'I think the situation in Rhodesia is getting out of hand.' He cited as indications that Rhodesia is approaching the brink, frequent call-ups, constant shortages, announcements of 'all-out drives to wipe out the terrorist menace'. He added, 'You can't win by trying to fool the people into believing you're going to wipe out the terrorist menace once and for all by calling up reservists. It becomes difficult to fight for something you don't think has a hope of succeeding.'[113]

THE INTERNATIONAL TRUST FUND

President Nyerere was the first to propose a fund to compensate white Rhodesian emigrants. His idea, first mooted in 1975, was that a useful way of undermining Smith would be to assist the departure of whites who would prefer to leave if it were financially possible for them to do so. Nyerere's idea was directly contrary to British contingency plans designed to encourage whites to stay in Rhodesia. This is because the British feared a repetition of the experience in Mozambique and Angola whose economies were badly disrupted by the large-scale exodus of Portuguese doctors, technicians, industrialists and skilled workers at independence. British proposals were based on the Kenyan experience where a compensation fund had been set up for farmers on the White Highlands, though there the fund was linked to the Kenyatta Government's own economic planning and formed part of British aid to Kenya.

At the first talks between Vorster and Kissinger in Bavaria in June 1976, the SA Prime Minister came out strongly in favour of a fund to compensate white Rhodesians who wished to leave, or whose land and property might be nationalized. After that meeting Kissinger began to develop the idea of an International Trust Fund, whose resources would be banked outside Rhodesia to provide a greater element of confidence about how they would be used. A committee of US, British and South African representatives was set up to work on the details of the plan. In its final shape the Trust Fund was designed not just to provide funds to compensate whites, but to act as an international consortium to raise substantial amounts of foreign aid for Zimbabwe's independent government. As in Kenya, the Fund would enable the Zimbabwean government to pay for land or property taken over from whites, as well as help emigrants get compensation for what they were forced to leave behind. But an incentive to remain would be provided by increasing the rate of compensation for those who stayed on longer.

Kissinger talked optimistically of a fund of two billion dollars; this was later scaled down considerably. The Ford Administration formally approached Western European nations and Japan to become participants. West Germany and France both responded. President Carter endorsed the proposal for the Trust Fund before he took office in December 1976. On the strength of his support, Britain formally invited 25 countries to contribute up to $1.3 billion to the Fund. When Ivor Richard visited Rhodesia in January 1977, he assured a trade union delegation that a Trust Fund would be set up to guarantee the position of white Rhodesians in case of need.

FULL CIRCLE: SMITH'S SECOND UDI

Almost a year after Kissinger had set out in April 1976 to halt a race war and to prevent southern Africa becoming a cockpit for international rivalry, the situation was more ominous than before the start of his mission. No progress at all had been made towards resolving the crisis in Namibia; and Smith had declared his 'second UDI'—this time to implement unilaterally the settlement terms he had negotiated with Kissinger. Even should he succeed in getting enough blacks inside Rhodesia to co-operate in this effort, Smith would not get either African or international recognition for a 'majority rule' Interim Government masterminded by the Rhodesian Front. Vorster told him so when Smith went to seek his support for the plan on 9 February 1977—and Vorster, after all, is in a good position to offer this kind of advice, since his own plans to produce a similar settlement for Namibia and for the independence of the Transkei had run up against precisely the same problem of non-recognition by the international community. Smith has nevertheless gone on believing that the US would 'honour' the agreement reached with Kissinger. By refusing to negotiate seriously with the Africans at Geneva, Smith destroyed any chance of winning their co-operation; and by rejecting the amended proposals accepted by the UK, US, the FLPs and SA, he made it less likely than ever that he would get the kind of support he would need from abroad if his new plan were to succeed. Smith had in fact led Rhodesia back into the *cul de sac* from which Kissinger had seemed to rescue it. The resignation of the Rhodesian Minister of Defence, Reg Cowper, in February 1977 pointed up the Rhodesians' acute dilemma. The country had by then reached the stage where its economic and manpower resources were so stretched that a choice had to be made between calling up more white Rhodesians to keep the guerrillas at bay, or keeping them at work to prevent the economy from collapsing under the combined pressures of economic sanctions and the growing burden of the defence costs. Cowper insisted that the first priority should be to increase military manpower; Smith took the side of those concerned with defending the economy. The conclusion is inescapable: without a settlement, Rhodesia cannot survive.

SA's dilemma also remains. It desperately needs to stop the war in Rhodesia, but Vorster is unwilling to apply the necessary pressures on the Smith regime, a position he reiterated when speaking in his Parliament on 28 January 1977. Without a settlement in Rhodesia he is not ready to move towards a radical settlement for the Namibian crisis. And without that the fighting will escalate there—with Angola becoming the base country for Swapo, as Mozambique is for Zipa, but with an even greater risk of active foreign involvement on the Namibian front.

After the failure of the Richard initiative, Britain's Foreign Secretary told Parliament (25 January 1977) that the chances of 'armed Marxist' participation in Rhodesia had been greatly increased, bringing with it the danger of Russian and Cuban intervention in the conflict. The urgent need, he argued, was for yet another Anglo-American diplomatic initiative.

The US Administration's position, stated by the Secretary of State, Cyrus Vance, on 10 February 1977, was that 'under no circumstances can the Rhodesian authorities count on any form of American assistance in their effort to prevent majority rule in Rhodesia', or for their efforts to enter into negotiations which 'exclude leaders of the nationalist movements'. He added that Washington still remained committed to finding a peaceful alternative to war in co-operation with

Britain, SA and the African leaders.

The FLPs, while still not closing their minds finally to the need for further diplomatic efforts, have grown even less confident of diplomacy than when they first welcomed the Kissinger and, later, the Ivor Richard initiatives. They saw no way that diplomacy could succeed unless—as Nyerere told the US Ambassador to the UN, Andrew Young, on 6 February 1977—Smith was 'ousted'. He thought this objective could be assisted by further tightening the economic pressures on Rhodesia. While not ruling out the value of further diplomatic efforts, their own priorities were to help intensify the armed struggle of both Zipa and Swapo, and to assist Mozambique in the defence of its borders.

The OAU secretary-general, William Eteki Mboumoua, proposed in January 1977 that a pan-African military force should be stationed in Mozambique, Angola and Zambia. This idea had previously been discussed with Nigeria during state visits made by the Presidents of Tanzania and Zambia. The creation of such an African border force was explored at the meeting of the OAU Liberation Committee in Lusaka at the end of January 1977, making the prospect of African military involvement along the borders of Rhodesia and Angola come into realistic focus for the first time. Such a force is likely to reduce the risks of non-African powers becoming involved, but it would also mark a further notch up the scale of military involvement in the southern African struggle.

The recognition accorded by the FLPs to the Patriotic Front (subsequently endorsed by the OAU) gave them a sharp edge over Muzorewa's ANC, thus sharpening the rivalry between them. The ANC believe that they not only command overwhelming majority support inside the country, but also that they have a considerable following inside Zipa, which (for reasons already explained) remains inarticulate. Their future tactics must be dictated by the immediate advantage they hold inside their constituency at home. They have been left as the only African movement with whom the Smith regime could still negotiate. So, at one level, the ANC was weakened by the FLPs' decision; but at a different level, they were left in a stronger position to initiate any new negotiations that might take place with the Smith regime. The implications of the continuing rivalries among Zimbabweans therefore remain serious for the future.

THE RUSSIANS' RINGSIDE SEAT

'The Soviet Union's stand on the problems of southern Africa is clear and definite: the Soviet Union has no, and cannot have, any "special interests", neither in south nor north, nor in any other part of Africa. The USSR does not look for any benefits for itself there. It only strives for the sacred right of every people to decide its own destiny, for the right to choose its own way of development. This is our unwavering principle, which the Soviet people will never abandon.'—Yuri Kornilov, in *Tass,* 11 October 1976

The Russians' successful military intervention with the Cubans in Angola[114] strengthened their influence in southern Africa, but they failed to follow up their success in the immediate post-Angolan phase. This, possibly short-term, setback can be attributed to five different factors. The most crucial was the FLPs' determination to avoid international military involvement in Rhodesia and Namibia if at all possible. This wish to avoid foreign entanglements does not rule out military support for the liberation movements from any quarter—subject only to all arms being channelled exclusively through the OAU Liberation Committee in Dar es Salaam. In this way the FLPs can hope to control the flow of arms and prevent rival forces being sustained by outside Powers, as happened in Angola. The second factor was the FLPs' strong preference for a peaceful rather than a violent settlement of the crises in Rhodesia and Namibia: this preference led to their decision to co-operate with Kissinger. The third factor was the diplomatic momentum set up by Kissinger, which left the Russians fulminating on the sidelines against what their Foreign Minister, Andrei Gromyko, termed 'political gimmickry'. (This charge of 'mere gimmickry' could equally be applied to the FLPs since their role was essential to Kissinger's diplomacy.) The fourth factor was Zanu's refusal to accept a Russian role in their military camps since this would have meant breaking with the Chinese with whom their military cadres have worked closely for ten years. As Zanu comprises by far the biggest element in Zipa, Moscow's urgings that Cubans be brought in as instructors in the use of Russian weapons could be resisted. Zanu's relations with the Chinese had earlier led the Russians to adopt Nkomo's Zapu as their favourite (see above). However, Zapu's cadres had been mostly trained in Eastern Europe, and there were no Russian surrogates in the Zapu camps in Tanzania. What remains unclear is how Zanu/Zapu co-operation in the Patriotic Front and in Zipa's Joint Command will affect their relations with Peking and Moscow. The Chinese, who speak of the Cubans as 'Russian mercenaries', successfully took a strong stand against any of Castro's military instructors being brought into the same camps as themselves. The final factor was Swapo's strong wish to remain strictly non-aligned. Although the instructors in their own camps are Chinese, their leaders have carefully avoided taking sides in Sino/Soviet disputes. However, Swapo began seriously to re-examine its options in 1976 and appears to have moved closer to taking up the Russian offer for reasons already explained (see The Fourth Front above).

Kissinger's diplomacy produced two quandaries for the Russians. Until the Secretary of State made his Lusaka speech in April 1976 announcing the new US policy towards southern Africa, Moscow could—with considerable justification —hold up the Americans as supporters of the white-ruled regimes, and especially of SA. It became much harder to do this after the US commitment to work for majority rule throughout the region. Moscow's propaganda in Africa therefore concentrated on trying to show that the Americans had not genuinely stopped being 'the patrons of the racialist regimes', but that they had simply changed their tactics to bolster up their 'Nato alliance' and to undermine the increasingly successful liberation movements. If Anglo-Americans were genuine in wishing to overthrow the 'racialist regimes' why, asked Moscow, did they not use their power to remove them? The Soviets' warning to Africa was that the Nato partners remained primarily interested in preserving the position of the 'imperialist monopolies' in Rhodesia and SA; and that this explained their 'slandering policy' against the Soviets—'the African people's most faithful allies'.[115] The answer to these manoeuvres, said Moscow, was to establish 'a united anti-imperialist front of African states'.[116]

It was easier for the Russians to criticize the 'hypocrisy and duplicity of the imperialists' than it was to explain why the FLPs had worked with Kissinger. Why had Nyerere and his colleagues not seen that Kissinger's shuttle diplomacy was, as *Pravda* described it (16 September 1976), 'a dangerous plot between imperialists and racists?' Was it because the 'collusion' was going on behind the Africans' backs, or because of the imperialist 'pressures' on African leaders?[117] In other words were the Russians really saying that Nyerere, Kaunda, Machel and Khama were too stupid to see the 'plot' for themselves, or that they were too weak to resist the 'imperialist pressures'? These were the logical conclusions to be drawn from the Soviet analysis of the implications of Kissinger's diplomacy, but of course they were never openly referred to in Moscow's broadcasts to Africa, which were always careful to avoid the slightest hint of criticism of the FLPs. Nor was there any attempt to report or analyse the African leaders' reasons for working with Kissinger.

It would be a serious mistake, though, to suppose that despite the Soviets' failure to gain any significant advantage from their Angolan achievement, they might not yet succeed in their objectives. Among advances they could claim in 1976 was the consolidation of their relations with Angola through the Friendship Treaty.[118] Machel, an old friend of China, went on a 'friendship visit' to Moscow, and began to show interest in closer Russian military relations if the South Africans should become involved in Rhodesia. Swapo had also moved somewhat closer to accepting the Russian offer of military support. The pro-Moscow groupings in the SA liberation movement became more effective from their new operational headquarters in Mozambique.[119] If the Western diplomatic initiative should fail in the end, the Russians will almost certainly be the foreign power most likely to benefit. The visit of President Podgorny to southern Africa in March 1977 showed that the Russians remain closely interested in the future of the sub-continent.

The Chinese, in sharp contrast to the very active role they played in the Angolan affair,[120] kept an extremely low profile in Mozambique and Rhodesia, while sustaining their customary attacks on the 'modern tsars'. Their present activities have been confined to maintaining their training presence in the guerrilla camps.

The Cuban role in Mozambique and Rhodesia appears to have been greatly exaggerated in 1976. Their numbers in Mozambique were variously estimated at between 500 and 1,000 by the Rhodesians and South Africans. A much likelier estimate is between 100 and 200 Cubans working mainly as technicians, doctors and skilled workers for the Maputo government. They do not seem to be directly involved in the military struggle—not yet—at any rate. However, their interest in the area remains keen, as was shown by Fidel Castro's whirlwind tour of the area in March 1977.[121]

NOTES

All newspaper references are to British papers unless otherwise indicated. References to 'this volume' and 'Documents section' relate to 1976-7 edition of *Africa Contemporary Record*.

1. See *Africa Contemporary Record (ACR)* 1974-5; pp. A3ff, A94ff. Also *ACR* 1975-6, pp. A118ff, C97ff.
2. See *ACR* 1974-5, pp. A69ff, B527ff.
3. See *ACR* 1975-6, 'Foreign intervention in Angola', pp. A3-38.
4. Interview with Julius Nyerere, Thames TV, 23 September 1976.
5. *Ibid.*
6. *Ibid.*
7. See *ACR* 1974-5, 'SA: the Secret Diplomacy of Detente', pp. A8ff; *ACR* 1975-6, pp. A39ff.
8. *Ibid.*
9. *ACR* 1975-6, pp. A49ff.
10. *Ibid*, pp. A47ff.
11. *ACR* 1974-5, pp. A8, A11f. *ACR* 1975-6, pp. A48f, B639, C75.
12. See article by the author 'Rhodesia on Verge of All-Out War' in *The Observer*, 15 February 1976. The 'authoritative Zambian spokesman' quoted was in fact President Kaunda.
13. Speech to the Royal Commonwealth Society, London; 19 February 1976.
14. For statement see Documents Section p. 162.
15. *Financial Times,* 27 February 1976.
16. *Daily Telegraph,* 27 February 1976.
17. See chapter on Mozambique in this volume.
18. *The Observer*, 7 March 1976.
19. For the terms see Documents Section, pp. C161f.
20. *The Times*, 5 April 1976.
21. See essay on 'The OAU in 1976' in this volume.

22. See *ACR* 1974-5, pp. A7ff.
23. In an interview with David Martin, *The Observer,* 7 March 1976.
24. *Zambia Daily Mail*, Lusaka, 29 April 1976.
25. *The Star*, Johannesburg, 24 April 1976.
26. See *ACR*, 1969-70, pp. C41ff.
27. See *ACR,* 1974-5, pp. A12ff.
28. *Radio Maputo*, 28 January 1977.
29. See *ACR,* 1971-2, pp. C144ff; 1972-3, pp. C139ff.
30. See David Martin's account in *The Observer*, 7 March 1976.
31. See *ACR* 1975-6, p. B386.
32. *The Zimbabwe Star*, 12 June 1976.
33. *Chimurenga: Zanu Monthly Newsletter*, 1:6 (31 May 1976).
34. *Daily Telegraph*, 7 October 1976.
35. Interview with the author.
36. *Daily Telegraph,* 19 October 1976.
37. *Rhodesian Herald*, Salisbury, 1 December 1976.
38. *Ibid*, 4 December 1976.
39. *Ibid.*
40. *Ibid*, 6 December 1976.
41. *Ibid.*
42. *The Times,* 27 November 1976.
43. *Ibid*, 10 September 1976.
44. Radio Maputo, 22 January 1977.
45. See chapter on Rhodesia in this volume.
46. E. Sutton-Pryce, Deputy Minister in the Prime Minister's office; *Financial Times*, 26 January 1977.
47. *The Times*, 21 January 1977.
48. Peter Younghusband in the *Daily Mail*, 13 December 1976.
49. *Ibid.*
50. *Ibid.*
51. Interview with the author.
52. John Edwards in the *Daily Mail*, 16 October 1976.
53. *Daily Telegraph*, 4 October 1976.
54. See chapter on South Africa in this volume.
55. See note 7.
56. See 'International Involvement in Angola,' *ACR* 1975-6, pp. A3ff.
57. See under Sport in chapter on SA in this volume.
58. *Rand Daily Mail*, Johannesburg, 15 November 1975.
59. See chapter on SA in this volume.
60. See *ACR* 1975-6, p. C71.
61. See chapter on Namibia in this volume.
62. See *ACR* 1975-6, pp. B556ff.
63. See chapter on Transkei in this volume.
64. See *ACR* 1974-5, pp. A93ff.
65. See *ACR* 1974-5, pp. A87-101; 1975-6, pp. A120ff.
66. See Documents Section, pp. C157.
67. Quoted by Bernard Gwertzman, *New York Times*, 8 September 1976.
68. *The Times*, 18 May 1976.
69. This and subsequent notes from Kissinger's conversations come from a number of sources close to him during his shuttle.
70. Interview with Bridget Bloom, *Financial Times*, 11 September 1976.
71. *The Guardian*, 15 September 1976.
72. Interview with David Martin, *The Observer*, 5 September 1976.
73. See chapter on Rhodesia in this volume.
74. Radio Salisbury, 27 August 1976.
75. *Ibid.*
76. *The Times*, 3 September 1976.
77. *Daily Telegraph*, 16 August 1976.
78. Part of this account appeared previously in *The Observer,* 26 September 1976.
79. For details, see Documents section, p. C157.
80. *The Guardian*, 29 June 1977.
81. *International Herald Tribune*, Paris, 20 November 1976.
82. *Ibid*, 15 October 1976.
83. *Ibid,* 20 November 1976.

84. *New York Times*, 16 November 1976.
85. *The Guardian*, 29 January 1977.
86. Murray Marder, *International Herald Tribune*, Paris, 28 September 1976.
87. *The Guardian*, 28 January 1977.
88. *Ibid*, 29 January 1977.
89. For details of proposal announced by Smith, see Documents Section, p. C157.
90. For full text of FLPs commonuique, see Documents section, p. C158.
91. Radio Havana, 27 September 1976.
92. Radio Maputo, 5 October 1976.
93. Full statement broadcast by Radio Maputo, 30 September 1976.
94. Radio Kampala, 30 August 1976.
95. *The Times*, 1 October 1976.
96. See chapter on Mozambique in this volume.
97. See chapter on Zambia in this volume.
98. Henry Kamm (*International Herald Tribune,* Paris, 14 October 1976) quoting a Government source, reported that Salisbury 'holds it more than likely that the talks will stalemate because of "posturing" and mutual "outbidding" by the Nationalist spokesmen.'
99. The agreed formula was: 'It is the British Government's firm position that all the agreed processes in Rhodesia will be completed in time to enable independence to be granted by 1 March 1978. The British Government therefore fix 1 March 1978 as the latest date by which Rhodesia will become independent and on this basis independence could come even by 1 December 1977. Before the conclusion of the conference and after agreeing on the establishment of the interim Government, the conference will revert to the question of fixing a date for independence so that a firm date can be agreed upon.' *The Observer*, 28 November 1976.
100. *Rhodesia Herald*, 22 November 1976.
101. *Ibid*, 25 November 1976.
102. See Bridget Bloom in *The Financial Times*, 12 November 1976.
103. *The Guardian*, 18 November 1976.
104. e.g. House of Commons debates, 21 October 1976. *The Times,* 18 September 1976.
105. *The Times*, 25 January 1977.
106. *Daily Telegraph*, 26 January 1977.
107. *The Times*, 25 January 1977.
108. See chapter on Angola in this volume.
109. *International Herald Tribune*, Paris, 10 December 1976.
110. *Daily Dispatch,* East London (SA), 22 December 1976.
111. *The Times*, 11 February 1977.
112. *International Herald Tribune*, Paris, 10 December 1976.
113. *The Star*, Johannesburg, 24 July 1976.
114. For relations between Moscow and Havana, see essay on Cuba in Africa in this volume.
115. Vladimir Petrov, Radio Moscow, 30 September 1976.
116. *Ibid*, 7 September 1976.
117. Boris Kalyagin, Radio Moscow, 14 September 1976.
118. See Documents section, pp. C151ff.
119. See chapter on South Africa in this volume.
120. See *ACR* 1975-6, pp. A3ff.
121. See note 114 above.

DOCUMENTS

RHODESIA

Statement issued by the African National Council
after the Breakdown of Constitutional Talks in Salisbury

19 March 1976

The African National Council (ANC) believes that the issues between it and the Rhodesian Front (RF) should be clearly stated at this stage in order that there should be no misunderstanding. The following points appear to state the position:

1. The RF has rejected majority rule now. It has accepted the principle of majority rule, but in some indefinite future, too far ahead to be accepted by the ANC.

2. Assuming that an acceptable settlement is agreed, the RF has proposed immediate parity in Cabinet but not in Parliament.

3. The RF has put forward a proposal for a three-tier assembly, in which a third of the seats would be European, a third African, and a third national seats on a common roll, with a high qualification.

4. This arrangement would ensure a European majority of two-thirds, or nearly that, at first and a European majority of some kind for an indefinite period. There are differences of opinion about how long it would be, but it would certainly be far longer than the ANC can contemplate. The RF thinks that it would be from 10 to 15 years.

5. The ANC's strong conviction is that there would be no racial rolls and that the proper franchise is one man one vote on one common roll. But to meet European fears, which the ANC believe to be unfounded, the ANC will reluctantly be prepared to consider, as part of an over-all settlement and in a spirit of compromise, that, in addition to the national seats, there should be European and African seats, but would require the African seats to be elected by universal adult suffrage. It is understood that the RF will accept this.

6. But the ANC insists on the qualifications on the middle or national roll being in substance no higher than those for the 'B' roll in the ANC's proposals.

7. The RF has rejected this on the ground that it would lead to majority rule at the first election.

8. Both sides accept that, as part of an over-all settlement, there should be an interim government on a national basis. On its length, the difference between the parties is that the ANC believes that the period should be short: 12 months. The RF believes that it should be part of an evolutionary change to majority rule over an indefinite period as explained above. The ANC believes that this is wrong in principle and dangerous in practice. It is in the interests of the whole nation that the period should be short so that all can turn to build the new nation and forget the dangerous frustrations of the past, which would continue during any long interim period.

9. On the structure of the interim government, the ANC has pointed out that it would be impracticable and valueless to have parity in the Cabinet, as suggested by the RF, whilst having a Parliament dominated by a European minority (*sic*).

10. The RF's argument to meet this objection is: that there would be a national government; the ANC and the RF would go to the country on a national policy; there would be an agreement whereby half the Cabinet would be Africans; and the Cabinet has the sole right to introduce legislation, so that it could control a possible hostile European majority in Parliament.

11. These arguments are fallacious. Parliament is not confined to considering government legislation only. Members can introduce Bills. They can refuse supply. Parliament would control the situation even against a majority in the Cabinet.

12. It is impossible for the ANC to accept the African position under such a situation. As Joshua Nkomo said, the Africans would be hostages.

13. The ANC requires effective parity in an interim government as a step to majority rule as soon as the necessary arrangements can be made under the new constitution; namely within 12 months. The ANC believes that this is in the true interest of all. It believes that, over the short period of such an interim government, it should take the form of an executive council, with legislative powers on which there would be parity. There is nothing legally impossible or impracticable in this. It is a matter of getting the necessary legislation through the UK and Rhodesian Parliaments.

14. The RF is unwilling to consider government without a Parliament. A Parliament may be necessary over a long period of transition, but not over the short period of 12 months envisaged by the ANC.

15. Again, in a spirit of compromise, the ANC would be prepared to consider some form of legislature even in the short term of 12 months, as long as there was equal representation.

16. The ANC could not accept a position in which it had parity in the interim Cabinet and reverted to a minority position in Parliament under the new constitution. Parity would have to lead to majority rule.

17. In summary the differences are the period before majority rule and the character of the interim government. But the latter will fall into place once there is agreement on the former. Most of the differences on this point arise from different views about the length of the interim period.

18. The ANC puts the following questions to the RF: assuming an agreement on an independence constitution do you accept:

(a) the principle of an immediate interim parity government, both in the executive and the legislature?

(b) that, at the end of the interim period, there must be majority rule?

(c) if so, what is the minimum period you would agree?

It is clear from the above that the answer to questions (a) and (b) is 'no' and question (c) does not arise.

Source: The Times, London, 20 March 1976.

British Plan to End Rhodesia Crisis

*Statement by the British Foreign Secretary
in the House of Commons, 22 March 1976*

The Foreign Secretary, Mr Callaghan, reported to the House of Commons on 22 March 1976 that Britain had proposed a two-stage plan to end the Rhodesian crisis and would consider financial and other means to this end. On the first stage there must be prior agreement by all the principal parties of a number of pre-conditions.

He said that this first stage involved four points:

(1) acceptance of majority rule;

(2) elections for majority rule within 18 months to two years;

(3) no independence before majority rule;

(4) no long drawn out negotiations.

If these pre-conditions were agreed the second stage of negotiating the actual terms of an independence constitution could begin.

Mr Callaghan said it would then be possible to reach a settlement which would go a very long way towards reconciling 'African aspirations and European fears'. He added that Britain would be prepared to play a constructive part in any negotiations and be willing to sit down with representatives of all shades of Rhodesian opinion inside and outside that country.

Mr Callaghan said an independent Rhodesia would need development assistance and aid for educational and other purposes 'on a significant scale'. Britain would play her part but he called on the Common Market, Commonwealth countries and others to help.

Mr Callaghan added: 'In a final settlement achieved along these lines all should be ready to agree that guerrilla activity should cease and that an approach could be made to the UN with a view to lifting the economic sanctions now in force.'

Source: The *Guardian,* London, 23 March 1976.

EEC Resolution on Rhodesia adopted at Summit Meeting in Luxembourg

2 September 1976

The Summit adopted a Dutch-sponsored declaration affirming 'the right of the Rhodesian people to self-determination and independence' and deploring 'the fact that recent events (in Salisbury) have made a peaceful transfer of power to the majority more difficult'.

The nine heads of government 'vigorously' supported the policy towards Rhodesia outlined by Mr Callaghan, the Foreign Secretary, in the House of Commons on 22 March. This called on Mr Smith, the Rhodesian Prime Minister, to hold elections on the basis of majority rule within two years.

The summit also appealed 'solemnly to the Rhodesian minority, which at present is opposing a system of majority rule, to accept a peaceful and rapid transition to such a system'. The leaders said they would continue to apply strictly UN Security Council decisions concerning Rhodesia (a reference to sanctions).

Source: The Times, London, 27 September 1976.

Text of Rhodesian Settlement Terms Announced 24 September 1976

Proposals put forward by US Secretary of State, as outlined by Rhodesian leader, Ian Smith

1. Rhodesia agrees to majority rule within two years.
2. Representatives of the Rhodesian government will meet immediately at a mutually agreed place with African leaders to organize an interim government to function until majority rule is implemented.
3. The interim government should consist of a Council of State, half of whose members will be black and half white with a white chairman without a special

vote. The European and African sides would nominate their representatives. Its function will include general supervisory responsibility for legislation and supervising the process of drafting the constitution.

The interim government should also have a Council of Ministers with a majority of Africans and an African first Minister. For the period of the interim government the Ministers of Defence and of Law and Order would be white. Decisions of the Council of Ministers to be taken by two-thirds majority. Its functions should include delegating legislative authority and executive responsibility.

4. The UK will enact enabling legislation for the process to majority rule. Upon enactment of that legislation Rhodesia will also enact such legislation as may be necessary to the process.

5. Upon the establishment of the interim government, sanctions will be lifted and all acts of war, including guerrilla warfare, will cease.

6. Substantial economic support will be made available by the international community to provide assurance to Rhodesians about the economic future of the country. A trust fund will be established outside Rhodesia which will organize and finance a major international effort to respond to the economic opportunities of this country and to the effects of the changes taking place. The fund will, *inter alia,* support the internal and external economic circumstances of the country and provide development assistance, guarantees and investment incentives to a wide variety of projects.

The aim will be to expand the industrial and mineral production of the country, to enhance agricultural potential by suitable land utilization and development programmes and to provide the necessary training and educational facilities to provide the essential flow of skills.

Proposals for Rhodesian Settlement, as Communicated to Rhodesian Nationalists

The detailed proposals for a Rhodesian settlement which the American Secretary of State, Dr Henry Kissinger, put to Rhodesian nationalists differ substantially from Mr Ian Smith's broadcast version of the plan, according to a document dated 21 September 1976. The proposals put to the Rhodesian nationalists were as follows:

1. Friday, 24 September 1976, Ian Smith will make a statement accepting majority rule within two years, as demanded by the British and the Americans. Before Friday, Smith is informing his Cabinet and his party caucus.

2. In his statement, Smith will invite black leaders (whoever they are) to come forward in order to form an interim or transitional government.

3. The structure of the transitional government will be as follows:

(a) Council of State consisting of an equal number of black and white representatives. The chairman of the Council of State should be white. The size of the Council of State can be as small as four (two nationalists and two whites) or it can be eight (four nationalists and four whites). The function of the Council will be like that of a governor-general or a high commissioner, as was in the case of Mozambique. The Council of State will supervise the drawing up of a constitution.

(b) A Council of Ministers consisting of a black Prime Minister and a majority of black Ministers. The Rhodesians specifically requested that they control the Ministries of Defence and Law and Order. The reason for this is the fear of a possible collapse of the administration during the period of transition. They refer to Angola, where arrests and counter-arrests finally led to the breakdown of government machinery.

4. Decisions will be by two-thirds majority of the Council of Ministers.

5. The rebel constitution will be suspended.
6. Britain will pass enabling legislation.
7. Once the transitional government is formed, the sanctions will have to be lifted and normality restored. Members of the Council of State will be chosen by each side, namely, the nationalists on one side and the whites on the other. This will apply to the members of the Council of Ministers.
8. The transitional government can be established as early as next month and independence within 24 months.

Source: The Observer, London, 3 October 1976.

Statement Issued by the Five Front-line Presidents (of Tanzania, Zambia, Mozambique, Botswana and Angola)

Lusaka, 26 September 1976

The struggle of the people of Zimbabwe, the African and international solidarity in the implementation of sanctions and co-ordinated action of all anti-colonialist forces and States have together brought the isolation and collapse of the illegal racist minority regime in the British colony of Southern Rhodesia.

The Presidents hailed and congratulated the people and fighters of Zimbabwe whose hard and heroic armed struggle forced the rebel regime and the enemy in general to recognize and accept the inevitability of majority rule, the need to establish immediately a transitional government to implement this principle. Thus the victories achieved by the people of Zimbabwe in their armed struggle created the present favourable conditions for the convening of a constitutional conference.

This is a victory for all Africa and mankind and particularly for all those countries and peoples who made sacrifices so that the brotherly people of Zimbabwe can be free.

Now that the pressures of armed struggle have forced the enemy to accept majority rule as a condition for immediate independence, the five Presidents call upon the colonial authority, the British Government, to convene at once a conference outside Zimbabwe with the authentic and legitimate representatives of the people:

(a) to discuss the structure and functions of the transitional government.
(b) to establish the transitional government.
(c) to discuss the modalities for convening a full constitutional conference to work out the independence constitution.
(d) to establish the basis upon which peace and normalcy can be restored in the territory.

To achieve these goals two phases are envisaged. The first phase will deal with the establishment of an African majority transitional government. The second phase will be concerned with working out the details of the Zimbabwe independence constitution.

The Presidents have carefully studied the proposals as outlined by the illegal and racist regime which, if accepted, would be tantamount to legalizing the colonialist and racist structures of power. Any details relating to the structure and functions of the transitional government should be left to the conference.

The five Presidents reaffirmed their commitment to the cause of liberation in Zimbabwe and the armed struggle. A luta continua (the struggle continues).

Source: The Times, London; 3 September 1976.

UNITED STATES AND AFRICA

Official Text of US Secretary of State Henry Kissinger's
Lusaka Statement, including the US Ten-point Policy on Rhodesia

Speech delivered at State House, Lusaka, Zambia, 27 April 1976

I have come to Africa because in so many ways, the challenges of Africa are the challenges of the modern era. Morally and politically, the drama of national independence in Africa over the last generation has transformed international affairs. More than any other region of the world, Africa symbolizes that the previous era of world affairs—the colonial era—is a thing of the past. The great tasks you face—in nation-building, in keeping the peace and integrity of this continent, in economic development, in gaining an equitable role in world councils, in achieving racial justice—these reflect the challenges of building a humane and progressive world order.

I have come to Africa with an open mind and an open heart to demonstrate my country's desire to work with you on these great tasks. My journey is intended to give fresh impetus to our co-operation and to usher in a new era in American policy . . . America's responsibilities as a global power give us a strong interest today in the independence, peace and well-being of this vast continent comprising a fifth of the world's land surface. For without peace, racial justice and growing prosperity in Africa, we cannot speak of a just international order.

There is nothing to be gained in a debate about whether in the past America has neglected Africa or been insufficiently committed to African goals. The US has many responsibilities in the world. Given the burden it has carried in the post-war period, it could not do everything simultaneously. African nations too have their own priorities and concerns, which have not always accorded with our own. No good can come of mutual recrimination. Our differing perspectives converge in a common purpose to build a secure and just future for Africa. In active collaboration there is much we can do; in contention or apart we will miss great opportunities. President Ford, the American Government and people are prepared to work with you with energy and goodwill if met in the same spirit.

So it is time to put aside slogans and to seek practical solutions. It is time to find our common ground and act boldly for common ends.

Africa is a continent of hope—a modern frontier. The US from the beginning has been a country of the frontier, built by men and women of hope. The American people know from their history the meaning of the struggle for independence, for racial equality, for economic progress, for human dignity . . .

Of all the challenges before us, of all the purposes we have in common, racial justice is one of the most basic. This is a dominant issue of our age, within nations and among nations. We know from our own experience that the goal of racial justice is both compelling and achievable. Our support for this principle in southern Africa is not simply a matter of foreign policy, but an imperative of our own moral heritage . . .

Here in Lusaka, I reaffirm the unequivocal commitment of the US to human rights, as expressed in the principles of the UN Charter and the Universal Declaration of Human Rights. We support self-determination, majority rule, equal rights and human dignity for all the peoples of southern Africa—in the name of moral principle, international law and world peace.

On this occasion I would like to set forth more fully American policy on some of the immediate issues we face—in Rhodesia, Namibia and SA—and then to sketch our vision of southern Africa's hopeful future.

DOCUMENTS

The US Position on Rhodesia

The US position on Rhodesia is clear and unmistakable. As President Ford has said, 'the US is totally dedicated to seeing to it that the majority becomes the ruling power in Rhodesia.' We do not recognize the Rhodesian minority regime. The US voted for, and is committed to the UN Security Council resolutions of 1966 and 1968 that imposed mandatory economic sanctions against the illegal Rhodesian regime. Earlier this year we co-sponsored a Security Council resolution, which was passed unanimously, expanding mandatory sanctions. And in March of this year, we joined with others to commend Mozambique for its decision to enforce these sanctions even at great economic cost to itself.

It is the responsibility of all who seek a negotiated solution to make clear to the Rhodesian minority that the world community is united in its insistence on rapid change. It is the responsibility of those in Rhodesia who believe in peace to take the steps necessary to avert a great tragedy.

US policy for a just and durable Rhodesian solution will therefore rest on ten elements:

First, the US declares its support in the strongest terms for the proposals made by British Prime Minister Callaghan on 22 March of this year: that independence must be preceded by majority rule which, in turn, must be achieved no later than two years following the expeditious conclusion of negotiations. We consider these proposals a basis for a settlement fair to all the people of Rhodesia. We urge that they be accepted.

Second, the Salisbury regime must understand that it cannot expect US support either in diplomacy or in material help at any stage in its conflict with African States or African liberation movements. On the contrary, it will face our unrelenting opposition until a negotiated settlement is achieved.

Third, the US will take steps to fulfil completely its obligation under international law to mandatory economic sanctions against Rhodesia. We will urge the Congress this year to repeal the Byrd Amendment, which authorizes Rhodesian chrome imports to the US—an act inconsistent with sanctions. In parallel with this effort, we will approach other industrial nations to ensure the strictest and broadest international compliance with sanctions.

Fourth, to ensure that there are no misperceptions on the part of the leaders of the minority in Rhodesia, the US, on the conclusion of my consultations in Black Africa, will communicate clearly and directly to the Salisbury regime our view of the urgency of a rapid negotiated settlement leading to majority rule.

Fifth, the US Government will carry out its responsibility to inform American citizens that we have no official representation in Rhodesia nor any means of providing them with assistance or protection. American travellers will be advised against entering Rhodesia; Americans resident there will be urged to leave.

Sixth, as in the case of Zambia a few years ago, steps should be taken—in accordance with the recent UN Security Council resolution—to assist Mozambique, whose closing of its borders with Rhodesia to enforce sanctions has imposed upon it a great additional economic hardship. In accordance with this UN resolution, the US is willing to provide $12.5 m of assistance.

Seventh, the US—together with other members of the UN—is ready to help alleviate economic hardship for any countries neighbouring Rhodesia which decide to enforce sanctions by closing their frontiers.

Eighth, humanitarian provision must be made for the thousands of refugees who have fled in distress from Rhodesia into neighbouring countries. The US will consider sympathetically requests for assistance for these refugees by the UN High Commissioner for Refugees or other appropriate international organizations.

Ninth, the world community should give its support to the people of Rhodesia as they make the peaceful transition to majority rule and independence, and should aid a newly independent Zimbabwe. To this end, we are ready to join with other interested nations in a programme of economic, technical and educational assistance, to enable an independent Zimbabwe to achieve the progress and the place in the community of nations to which its resources and the talents of all its people entitle it.

Finally, we state our conviction that whites as well as blacks should have a secure future and civil rights in a Zimbabwe that has achieved racial justice. A constitutional structure should protect minority rights together with establishing majority rule. We are prepared to devote some of our assistance programmes to this objective.

In carrying out this programme we shall consult closely with the Presidents of Botswana, Mozambique, Tanzania and Zambia.

We believe these are important measures. We are open-minded with respect to additional actions that can help speed a resolution. The US will consult closely with African leaders, especially the four Presidents, and with other friends on the Rhodesian problem. For the central fact that I have come here to stress is this: the US is wholly committed to help bring about a rapid, just and African solution to the issue of Rhodesia.

Namibia

Rhodesia is the most urgent but by no means the only critical problem in southern Africa. The Status of Namibia has been a source of contention between the world community and SA for over three decades.

The territory of South West Africa turned into a source of serious international discord following World War II. When the UN refused to accede to SA's proposal for annexation of the territory, SA declined to enter into a trusteeship agreement, and since then has refused to recognize the UN as the legal sovereign. In 1966, the General Assembly terminated SA's mandate over the territory. In 1971, the International Court of Justice concluded that SA's occupation of Namibia was illegal and that it should withdraw.

The US voted for the 1966 General Assembly resolution. We were the only major power to argue before the International Court that SA occupation was illegal. And in January 1976 the US voted in favour of the UN resolution condemning the occupation of Namibia and calling for SA to take specific steps toward Namibia's self-determination and independence.

We are encouraged by the SA Government's evident decision to move Namibia toward independence. We are convinced that a solution can be found which will embody equal rights for the entire population and at the same time protect the interests of all who live and work there. But we are concerned that SA has failed to announce a definite timetable for the achievement of self-determination; that all the people and all political groupings of Namibia have not been allowed to take part in determining the form of government they shall one day have. And that SA continues to deny the UN its proper role in establishing a free and independent Namibia.

Therefore the US position is as follows:

First, we reiterate our call upon the SA Government to permit all the people and groups of Namibia to express their views freely, under UN supervision, on the political future and constitutional structure of their country.

Second, we urge the SA Government to announce a definite timetable acceptable to the world community for the achievement of self-determination.

Third, the US is prepared to work with the international community, and especially with African leaders, to determine what further steps would improve prospects for a rapid and acceptable transition to Namibian independence. We are convinced that the need for progress is urgent.

Fourth, once concrete movement toward self-determination is underway, the US will ease its restrictions on trade and investment in Namibia. We stand ready to provide economic and technical assistance to help Namibia take its rightful place among the independent nations of the world.

South Africa

Apartheid in SA remains an issue of great concern to those committed to racial justice and human dignity.

No country, no people can claim perfection in the realm of human rights. We in America are aware of our own imperfections. But because we are a free society, our problems and our shortcomings are fully aired and made known to the world. And we have reason to take pride in our progress in the quest for justice for all in our country.

The world community's concern with SA is not merely that racial discrimination exists there. What is unique is the extent to which racial discrimination has been institutionalized, enshrined in law and made all-pervasive.

No one—including the leaders of Black Africa—challenges the right of white South Africans to live in their country. They are not colonialists; historically, they are an African people. But white South Africans must recognize as well that the world will continue to insist that the institutionalized separation of the races must end. The US appeals to SA to heed the warning signals of the past two years: there is still time to bring about a reconciliation of SA's peoples for the benefit of all. But there is a limit to that time—a limit of far shorter duration than was generally perceived even a few years ago.

A peaceful end to institutionalized inequality is in the interest of all South Africans. The US will continue to encourage and work for peaceful change. Our policy toward SA is based upon the premise that within a reasonable time we shall see a clear evolution toward equality of opportunity and basic human rights for all South Africans. The US will exercise all its efforts in that direction. We urge the Government of SA to make that premise a reality.

In the immediate future, the Republic of South Africa can show its dedication to Africa—and its potential contribution to Africa—by using its influence in Salisbury to promote a rapid negotiated settlement for majority rule in Rhodesia. This, we are sure, would be viewed positively by the community of nations as well as by the rest of Africa.

A Vision of the Future

Southern Africa has all the pre-requisites for an exciting future. Richly endowed with minerals, agricultural and hydroelectric potential, a favourable climate, and, most important, great human resources, it needs only to overcome the human failure of racial strife to achieve bright prospects for all its peoples.

Let us all strive to speed the day when this vision becomes a reality.

The US stands ready to work with the nations of southern Africa to help them achieve the economic progress which will give meaning to their political independence and dignity to their struggle for equality.